John E. Parnell

COMPUTER SCIENCE
Advanced Placement Guidebook

A SPECTRUM BOOK

PRENTICE-HALL, INC.
Englewood Cliffs, New Jersey 07632

Library of Congress Cataloging in Publication Data

Parnell, John E.
    Computer science advanced placement guidebook.

    "A Spectrum book."
    Bibliography: p.
    Includes index.
        1. Electronic digital computers—Programming—
Examinations, questions, etc.   2. PASCAL (Computer
program language)—Examinations, questions, etc.
I. Title.
QA76.28.P37   1985   001.64′2   84-18157
ISBN 0-13-163874-2
ISBN 0-13-163866-1 (pbk.)

10   9   8   7   6   5   4   3   2   1

Bookware® is a registered trademark of Prentice-Hall, Inc.

Editorial/production supervision by Jane Zalenski
Manufacturing buyer: Gary Orso

ISBN 0-13-163866-1 {PBK.}

ISBN 0-13-163874-2

PRENTICE-HALL INTERNATIONAL, INC., *London*
PRENTICE-HALL OF AUSTRALIA PTY. LIMITED, *Sydney*
PRENTICE-HALL CANADA INC., *Toronto*
PRENTICE-HALL HISPANOAMERICANA, S.A., *Mexico*
PRENTICE-HALL OF INDIA PRIVATE LIMITED, *New Delhi*
PRENTICE-HALL OF JAPAN, INC., *Tokyo*
PRENTICE-HALL OF SOUTHEAST ASIA PTE. LTD., *Singapore*
WHITEHALL BOOKS LIMITED, *Wellington, New Zealand*
EDITORA PRENTICE-HALL DO BRASIL LTDA., *Rio de Janeiro*

Contents

Introduction

This book was designed to bring together in a single location the concepts and techniques considered fundamental to an understanding of the field of computer science. The language used throughout this text is Pascal.

In May 1984, the College Entrance Examination Board began administering an annual examination in computer science. This book will aid the student in preparing for this Advanced Placement (AP) Examination. Throughout this book, there are numerous examples of questions that are of the difficulty level that you can expect to find in the AP Examination. Detailed solutions of all these questions are provided.

The Appendix of this book contains more information about the AP Examination. Included is a listing of the topical outline for the AP course in computer science as released by the College Board. By examining this outline, readers will be able to discover holes in their background in computer science, especially as it relates to their preparation for the AP Examination. Students can consult the appropriate area(s) within this book to fill in those holes.

GENERAL INFORMATION ABOUT THE ADVANCED PLACEMENT PROGRAM (APP)

What is the APP? The APP is a nonprofit venture set up by the Educational Testing Service (ETS) and the College Entrance Examination Board. Its purpose is to provide high school students the opportunity to demonstrate a college-level proficiency in any of a number of areas of academic endeavors.

Where are the AP Examinations given? During May of each year, the College Board administers examinations in these areas at a variety of test sites around the United States and abroad. Ask your high school guidance counselor for the location of the site nearest you.

How are the AP Examinations Scored? The score on the AP Examination ranges from 1 to 5. A general idea of the score's meaning follows.

> 5—Extremely well-qualified. A person earning this score is usually granted college credit for the examination.

> 4—Well-qualified. While not the best grade, a score of 4 on the examination also usually results in college credit.

> 3—Qualified. Colleges may or may not grant credit to students earning this score.

> 2—Possibly qualified. Most colleges will not grant credit for this score.

> 1—No recommendation. Like a score of 2, a score of 1 probably would not result in the granting of college credit.

THE AP COMPUTER SCIENCE COURSE

"The major emphasis in an AP computer science course is on programming methodology, algorithms, and data structures. Applications of computing provide the context in which these subjects are treated. Applications are used to develop student awareness of the need for particular algorithms and data structures, as well as to provide topics for programming assignments to which students can apply their knowledge. A particular programming language constitutes the vehicle for implementing computer-based solutions to particular problems. Treatments of computer systems and the social implications of computing are integrated into the course and not isolated as separate units."*

COURSE GOALS

1. "The student will be able to design and implement computer-based solutions to problems in several application areas.

2. "The student will learn well-known algorithms and data structures.

3. "The student will be able to develop and select appropriate algorithms and data structures to solve problems.

4. "The student will be able to code fluently in a well-structured fashion using an accepted high-level language. (The first offerings of the AP Computer Science Examination will require knowledge of Pascal).

5. "The student will be able to identify the major hardware and software

components of a company system, their relationship to one another, and the roles of these components within the system.

6. "The student will be able to recognize the ethical and social implications of computer use."*

ORGANIZATION OF THE AP EXAMINATION IN COMPUTER SCIENCE

The AP Examination in Computer Science is divided into two parts, which are each given equal weight in the determination of the overall score.

Part I consists of 45 objective multiple-choice questions. There is a 90-minute time limit on this part.

Since there is a penalty imposed for incorrect answers, it is usually not in your best interests to guess at an answer. The possible exception to this is if you are able to eliminate one or more of the suggested answers. When this is done, the chances are greater that you will "guess" the correct answer. Certainly, you are better off statistically.

Part II consists of from 5 to 10 free-response questions. In this part, you may be asked to write a program or answer an essay question. When writing programs in this part, the only acceptable language is Pascal. If you write the program in any other language, you get no credit.

Remember that the exam is not a test in Pascal programming, but rather a test in the concepts necessary to function effectively in computer science. Pascal is but the vehicle language for the examination. In future years, other languages may be acceptable on the examination. At present, however, you must use only Pascal.

One of the problems with Pascal is that, like many other computer languages, there exist several different dialects of the language. This is most unfortunate. This certainly will present the College Board with a problem with respect to grading the free-response section of the examination. The Readers have been instructed to use Standard Pascal syntax as the acceptable syntax. (Virtually no computer implements pure Standard Pascal. Some, though, can mimic Standard Pascal; OMSI Pascal is one example.) Most Pascal dialects use Standard Pascal as the basis for their compiler and then add to it various enhancements or improvements.

One solution to this problem is to have readers who are familiar with at least some of the major dialects. Another is to grade everybody against Standard Pascal and then to adjust the grades, since it is not the language being tested but rather the concepts of computer science. In preparing for the examination, it is best to check with your instructor for the latest word in this matter.

*Reprinted with permission from *Advanced Placement Course Description in Computer Science,* © 1984 by the College Entrance Examination Board, New York.

Problem Solving Procedures

PROBLEM SPECIFICATION

Before starting to write a computer program, you must have a clear concept of what the program is supposed to accomplish. The more specific the problem is, the better. Being asked to write a computer program to keep track of the circulation for a library is not specific enough. In being asked to write such a program, the following questions, among others, need to be answered:

1. What type of material will circulate? Books, records, art, tapes, etc.
2. For what type of borrower? Students, faculty, staff, etc.
3. Do different items or classes of items have different due dates?
4. Are penalties to be imposed for late returns?
5. May items be renewed?
6. Are records to be kept concerning such things as
   a. number of items borrowed by class of borrower
   b. number of items overdue/lost
   c. requests for items not available by reason of
      i. already being loaned out
      ii. not being owned at all
   d. amount of fines collected per class of borrower.

With thought, you should be able to come up with even more questions. The list is almost endless. From the above list, you can understand that the better the original problem specification (as well as the greater the functional specification), the easier it is to write a "good" program.

MODULARIZATION OF PROGRAMS

A great advantage of the Pascal language is that it can be modular in nature. That is, routines written for one program can be used in other programs. By writing programs in a modular fashion, it is easier to develop and debug each module since you need not be concerned with other parts of the program. Each module is the solution for a particular part of the programming assignment.

TOP-DOWN VERSUS BOTTOM-UP PROBLEM METHODOLOGY

Taking the main problem and breaking it down into successively smaller problems is called the top-down approach to writing programs. Basically, this involves a series of refinements into smaller and smaller problems, each of which is ultimately solved by a small program segment. The opposite of this is a bottom-up methodology.

STANDARDIZATION OF PROGRAMMING STYLE

Unfortunately, there is no generally accepted set of standards of programming style. As we learn to program, we develop our own style. If our programs are to be used by no one else, then it really doesn't matter what style we use, as long as we are consistent.

  If our programs are to be used for public consumption, then style does matter. Many large software houses have rules that must be followed when writing programs. This is also true for hardware manufacturers that also generate their own software (for example, DEC, IBM, CDC). Can you imagine the problems that would result if there was no uniform style, and you worked for six months on a project and then quit or were reassigned to another project, and another programmer was assigned to complete your job?

  All programmers do not work for major companies. Yet we must all write with clarity in mind. You can never tell when your program has a chance of being sold to someone else. Also, when a bug in a program surfaces, it is easier to debug if the programmer used a clear style.

Unlike some other computer languages, Pascal does not have line numbers. Consequently, we cannot reserve various sets of line numbers for specific purposes. So we have to use some other form of uniformity. Here are but a few suggestions that are used throughout this book.

Indentation

Be consistent when using indentation. With consistency comes clarity. Indent 2 to 3 spaces from the left margin when declaring the CONST, TYPE, VAR, PROCEDURE, and FUNCTION sections. Each of these sections should be indented so that they align, as they are of equal importance. The identifiers in the CONST, TYPE, and VAR sections should be indented another 2 to 3 spaces. The indentation for the BEGIN...END pair of the program body should be the same as that for the sections of the declaration portion of the program. The following is an illustration of the suggested indentation:

```
PROGRAM ...

  CONST
    ⟨identifier(s)⟩ : ⟨value(s)⟩;

  TYPE
    ⟨identifier(s)⟩ : ⟨type(s)⟩;

  VAR
    ⟨identifier(s)⟩ : ⟨type(s)⟩;

  PROCEDURE ...

  CONST

    ...

  TYPE

    ...

  VAR

    ...

  PROCEDURE ...
```

```
   ...
BEGIN
   ...
END;

  FUNCTION ...

    CONST
      ...

    TYPE
      ...

    VAR
      ...

    BEGIN
      ...
    END;

  BEGIN
    ...
  END.
```

Indentation and Conditional Statements

Indentation should also be used in conditional statements. The THEN and ELSE portions should each be indented 2 to 3 spaces from the IF portion. The THEN and ELSE portions should be aligned, as in the following illustration:

```
IF ...
   THEN ...

IF ...
   THEN ...
   ELSE ...
```

Other examples of suggested indentations are as follows:

```
FOR ...
   BEGIN
```

```
   ...
END

REPEAT
   ...
UNTIL ...

WHILE ...
   BEGIN
      ...
   END

CASE
   ...
END
```

Using Line Feeds

Use line feeds to increase clarity. Line feeds should be used to separate from one another the various sections in the declaration section of the program. A line feed should also separate the declaration section from the program heading and program body. The same can be said for using line feeds in PROCEDUREs and FUNCTIONs. This is illustrated on the previous page.

Choosing Identifiers

Care should be taken when choosing identifier names. The name used should give a clue as to its intended purpose in the program. For example, the identifiers FirstName and LastName are more indicative of their purpose in the program than the identifiers X and Y. The use of logical identifiers can help in program documentation and debugging. Be aware of the constraint that your compiler may place on you with respect to the maximum length of an identifier name. With a little planning, you should be able to use very long yet appropriate identifier names and still retain uniqueness.

Constants

Use constants whenever possible. This will allow you to change a single statement in a program, instead of having to hunt down several places whenever a change is necessary. For example, instead of defining a FOR loop as going from, say, 1 to 30, it would be better to define it as going from StartingValue to EndingValue. This way, if the size of the loop were to change, you would not have to find all the appropriate loops to make the change. You would merely have to change the values as specified in the CONST portion of the declaration section of the program.

The Declaration Precedence

List the various parts of the declaration section in the following order: CONST, TYPE, VAR, PROCEDURE, FUNCTION. Use this same order within each PROCEDURE and FUNCTION. Some compilers dictate this order. Since your program may have to run with a compiler different from the one originally intended, plan accordingly.

Comments

Use comments generously for program documentation. A one- or two-sentence comment should be used just after the program heading. This comment should briefly summarize the purpose of the program. Use a comment just after a PROCEDURE or FUNCTION heading, too. Each logical section of the program should have a brief comment describing its purpose.

Comments and Clarity

Whenever any unusual steps are taken in a program, they should be amply described in a comment. A general rule of thumb is: When there is a possibility of confusion, use a comment to improve clarity.

Comments and Reserved Words

Comments should also be used just after the reserved words BEGIN and END to indicate what you are beginning and ending. This is particularly important when more than one BEGIN...END pair is present.

TESTING COMPUTER PROGRAMS

Once a computer program has been written and before it is used by others, it should be tested by the programmer. This testing should include using data for which the output is already known. If the proper output is obtained, then you can feel better about the correctness of the program. If the output is incorrect, then the program needs more work.

When choosing test data, choose data that is representative of the type the program was designed for. Don't test an alphabetizing program with numbers; use words or names. Don't test an addition module with small numbers if the program is meant to keep track of a bank's assets.

ERRORS

No matter how hard a programmer tries to write error-free code, rare is the program that is written correctly the first time. Computer errors, called bugs, fall into any one of three types. These types are as follows: syntactical errors, logical errors, and run-time errors. Since errors will creep into even the best of programs, a brief discussion of these types of errors is warranted.

Syntactical Errors

Syntactical errors involve a violation of the grammatical rules of the programming language being used. They are the easiest type of error to make. Luckily, they are also the easiest type of error to detect and correct. They are so easy to detect that the "stupid" computer does the detection for us.

When a program is to be executed, a search for syntactical errors is performed by the compiler before it actually executes the program. Each programming language has its own clearly defined set of grammatical rules against which each and every line of code is compared. (The rules for Pascal are in the Appendix.) Remember that no matter how you write a program, the program must conform to these rules. You cannot change these rules through such artificial enhancements as indentation. Indentation is for humans, not machines.

You should be aware that there is not a single set of grammatical rules for any one language. Pascal is no exception. However, there is a set of standards for Pascal that does serve as a base line for most versions of Pascal. Indeed, all programs written with this standard in mind should execute successfully under all other versions. This standard is the ISO Standard Pascal.

Logic Errors

The most difficult type of error to detect is a logic error. Logic errors obey the rules of syntax, so they are not detected by the computer. Let's say that you have written a program to do some computations. You expect part of the output to be an eight, but instead you get a six. Where did you go wrong? Your program is more than 1100 lines long. Where do you begin? If the inputted values were four and two, you might initially suspect that somewhere these two values were added instead of multiplied. That would seem like a logical source of error. It would be easy to type " + " instead of "*".

Problem. Nowhere did you code multiplication. Where, then, is the source of your error? You have no choice but to hand trace the execution of your program; that is, you get to play computer. This is where comments and helpful variable names come to the rescue. If the program is modular, you can isolate and deal with each segment separately without being concerned with the rest of the program. By inserting WRITELN statements periodically throughout the module, you can compare the value the computer says a particular variable has with what you say it should have. This will help you narrow down the location of the error.

Run-time Errors

Run-time errors cause the computer program to "crash," that is, to end prematurely with an error message. There are many sources of run-time errors. These range from trying to divide by zero to trying to exceed MAXINT in an INTEGER variable and from trying to assign a REAL identifier a CHAR value to trying to use a subscript out of range.

It is best to plan for run-time errors, so that they don't surprise you. If you were to ask a question in the following manner, what do you think the possible responses would be?

"Do you wish to continue? (1 = Yes, 2 = No)"

Of course, logic would dictate a one or a two. What if someone were to type in a number greater than two? Or a decimal number? What about a Y or an N? That would never happen, you say. Think again. We don't always follow directions; "accidents" do happen. In this example, good programmers would never use an INTEGER variable for the response. They would plan for the possibility of a Y or an N, a Yes or No, a 3.2. The old adage, "An ounce of prevention is worth a pound of cure," holds true in computer programming.

EXERCISES

1–1. True or false. The development of a problem from the most generalized form to the specific form is called "top-down methodology."

1–2. The development of a program from its specific form to a more generalized form is called

  a. top-down methodology.

  b. bottom-up methodology.

  c. quick methodology.

  d. radix methodology.

  e. reasonable methodology.

1–3. Which of the following is the best way to make sure that the computer program being written is very clear?

    a. Use uniform rules of indentation.

    b. Write the program in a modular format.

    c. Make ample use of comments throughout the program.

    d. Choose identifier names that are descriptive of their function in the program.

    e. All of the above.

1–4. Which is the last statement that is repeated in the following loop?
BEGIN
FOR Counter := 1 TO 10 DO

    a. BEGIN

    b. SecondCounter := SecondCounter + 1;

    c. Alpha[SecondCounter] := Counter

    d. END;

    e. WRITELN ('Finished.')
END.

1–5. Which type of error manifests itself only when the computer compiles the program?

    a. Syntactical

    b. Logical

    c. Run-time

    d. Computer

    e. No errors are caught at the time of compilation.

1–6. Typing WRITELINE instead of WRITELN is an example of which type of error?

    a. Syntactical

    b. Logical

    c. Run-time

    d. Computer

    e. It's not an error; that is the proper way of telling the computer to write a line of type.

1–7. Typing "Counter := Counter − 1" instead of "Counter := Counter + 1" is which type of error?

    a. Syntactical

    b. Logical

    c. Run-time

    d. Computer

    e. No error, both statements are the same.

1–8. What is wrong with the following statement?
Counter + 1 = Counter

    a. There is no semicolon at the end of the line.

    b. The equal sign is not proper; it should be an assignment operator.

    c. The assignment statement is written backwards. It should have the computation on the right of the statement, not the left.

    d. All of the above corrections are needed.

    e. None of the above corrections are needed.

1–9. When a subscript in an array exceeds its original bounds, what type of error is generated?

    a. Syntactical

    b. Logical

    c. Run-time

    d. Computer

    e. No error is generated; only a warning message is generated.

1–10. An advantage of writing programs in a modular form is

    a. it is easier to debug a small module than the entire program at one time.

    b. modules may be written with one program in mind, yet may be applicable to other programs later.

    c. modules are easier to write, since they deal only with a small problem or function.

    d. all of the above.

    e. none of the above.

2

The Programming Language Pascal

GENERAL RULES

There are a few required parts of a program written in Pascal. They are:

Beginning a Program

Every program must start off with the reserved word PROGRAM. (Reserved words are words to which a specific meaning has been given. They can be used only in the manner intended. In this book, the reserved words are usually capitalized to show you that the word is a reserved word; sometimes, for ease of reading, the word appears in lowercase. Writing the word in lowercase does not change its meaning, however. For a complete list of reserved words, consult the Appendix.) The word PROGRAM signifies to the computer that that is the beginning of the Pascal program.

Identifiers

An identifier should follow the word PROGRAM. This identifier is the actual name of the program. An identifier must conform to the following rules.

1. It must start with a letter. It may, however, also contain numbers.
2. It may be virtually of any length. However, some compilers do set an upper limit. Typically, this limit is the length of an entire line. It is best to check the specific compiler being used before beginning. Certainly this is a great strength for Pascal. No longer is the pro-

grammer limited to a single letter or a single letter followed option- ally by a single-digit number. This allows for a form of internal documentation. For example, instead of using, say, "x" to represent the variable incremented to keep track of how many times a loop is executed, the identifier Loopcounter might be used.

3. Even though an identifier might be of any length, not every character may be examined for uniqueness. That is, given two identifiers that begin with the same characters but that end differently, the compiler may regard them as the same. For example, some compilers would regard the identifiers TemperatureCelsius and TemperatureFahren- heit as the same. Most often, only the first six or eight characters are examined for uniqueness. If this is the case with your compiler, then you will have to choose identifier names with greater care. Perhaps the two previous identifiers should have been CelsiusTemperature and FahrenheitTemperature.

   Judicious choosing of identifier names would greatly enhance the possibility of another person following the logic of one of your Pascal programs. Some compilers allow the underscore character (_) to be part of an identifier. This allows for even greater clarity, and it certainly allows for greater ease of reading. The previous iden- tifiers could then have been written as Celsius_Temperature and Fahrenheit_Temperature.

4. No character, other than alphanumerics (and possibly the under- score), can be used in an identifier. That is, no special characters (for example, $ and %), blanks, or spaces can be used.

Exercises

Which are valid user-defined identifiers?

2–1. John

2–2. Name

2–3. Name$

2–4. Ord

2–5. 1stHouse

2–6. First-Date

2–7. X%

2–8. My Name

2–9. Jim'sFriend

2–10. 3rdPlaceWinner

2–11. NameOfPerson

2–12. GameShow

Files

If files are going to be used in the program, then their names must follow the name of the program. The name(s) must be enclosed within parentheses. The format of file names must conform to the rules for naming identifiers. There are two files that have been assigned names already. These are for the keyboard and the screen. The keyboard and screen are files—special files. The names that have been assigned to these files are INPUT and OUTPUT, respectively. Therefore, if information is to be taken from the keyboard, then you must include the word INPUT into the program header. If information is to be written onto the screen, then you must also include the word OUTPUT.

Although the words INPUT and OUTPUT have been capitalized, they are not examples of reserved words. They are examples of standard identifiers. Like reserved words, standard identifiers have a meaning already assigned to them. Unlike reserved words, the meaning of standard identifiers may be changed. Most often, unless there is a pressing reason for doing otherwise, their meaning should not be changed. For a complete list of standard identifiers, consult the Appendix. Whenever more than one file is to be used by a program, the names of the files must be separated by commas.

Ending Statements

Following the right parenthesis (if files are being used) or following the name of the program (if files are not being used) must be a semicolon (;). In other words, the program header must end with a semicolon.

Beginning the Program Body

The next required part of a Pascal program is the reserved word BEGIN. This word signals to the compiler that this point is the beginning of the program body. The actual statements of the program are located within the program body. However, these statements are not required.

Ending the Program Body

The reserved word END followed by a period signals the end of not only the program body but also the end of the program itself. No statements following the period are recognized or executed.

FORMATTING A PROGRAM

Diagramatically, a Pascal program can be represented as follows.

```
PROGRAM ⟨identifier⟩ (⟨identifier⟩, ⟨identifier⟩, . . .);
  BEGIN
    ⟨statement⟩;
    ⟨statement⟩;
    . . .
    ⟨statement⟩
  END.
```

Note how this diagram was written. Each line in a Pascal program can be left justified, and one line can contain more than one statement. However, these methods are seldom used. Usually, each portion of the program is indented by a few spaces so you can more easily see which statements belong to which sections. The computer, however, disregards indentation altogether; it follows clearly defined rules to determine membership in a section. In writing programs, you must follow these rules, as well as write for clarity. For clarity, use only a single statement per line. Following are two other ways of writing the general format of a Pascal program. Neither of these, although each is syntactically correct, is very desirable.

```
PROGRAM ⟨identifier⟩ (⟨identifier⟩, ⟨identifier⟩, . . .);
BEGIN
⟨statement⟩;
⟨statement⟩;
. . .
⟨statement⟩
END.
```

```
PROGRAM ⟨identifier⟩ (⟨identifier⟩, ⟨identifier⟩, . . .);
BEGIN ⟨statement⟩; ⟨statement⟩; . . . ⟨statement⟩ END.
```

COMMENTS

Another way of increasing the clarity of a program is through the use of comments. Anywhere a space may be located, a comment may be placed. A comment is enclosed either within brace characters, { }, or within parenthesis-asterisk pairs, (*   *). (Note that there is no space between the parenthesis and the asterisk. A space would generate an error.) Quite often, a comment is placed after the declaration of a variable and at the beginning of and after the end of each section of the program. This book makes generous use of comments.

Unlike some other programming languages, Pascal executes anything located on a line after a comment. The following illustrates this point.

```
Sample (* dog food *) := 'Alpho';
```

assigns Alpho to the identifier Sample.

RESERVED WORDS

As has already been stated, a few words have been given a special meaning to start with. Thirty-five of these words are termed reserved words. The meaning of these words cannot be changed. A second set, consisting of 41 words, is termed standard identifiers. These have also been given previous meanings. However, their meaning can be changed within a program. Most often, it is ill-advised to redefine these words; there should be a pressing reason for doing so. A list of both the reserved words and standard identifiers is in the Appendix.

DECLARING VARIABLES

Prior to using an identifier for the first time, the computer must be informed as to its type. Predefined types include the following: BOOLEAN, CHAR, INTEGER, REAL, and ARRAY. The following is a brief discussion of these types.

BOOLEAN

BOOLEAN identifiers are to take on only a logical value. This value can only be TRUE or FALSE.

CHAR

Identifiers of type CHAR can take on a literal value. This value includes any legitimate character (for example, A to Z, 0 to 9, spaces, and special characters like % and $). This entire paragraph is composed of possible values for an identifier of type CHAR. (This entire paragraph cannot be assigned to one CHAR identifier. For the manner of assigning a paragraph to an identifier, see the section on ARRAYs.)

INTEGER

Numerical identifiers of type INTEGER are just that: integers. They are whole numbers—no fractional or decimal portions. They can be either positive or negative. There is both an upper limit and a lower limit to their magnitude. The upper limit is generally given in the form of the standard identifier MAXINT (standing for MAXimum INTeger). Quite often, this number is 32767. The lower limit is quite often − 32768. (The actual magnitude of this number depends on the number of bits used to represent a number and the location of the sign bit.)

REAL

Numbers larger than MAXINT or smaller than the smallest possible INTEGER can be represented as REAL numbers. REAL numbers can contain a decimal portion and can be either positive or negative. The magnitude of REAL numbers is also regulated by bits. For some systems, the largest REAL number may be 10**38, whereas the smallest may be 10** − 38. Just like INTEGER numbers, the magnitude of REAL numbers is controlled more by the hardware than by the software.

ARRAY

See Chapter 3 for a discussion of arrays.

Exercises

Indicate the proper type of identifier required for each of the following values.

2–13. 3.1415

2–14. John

2–15. 17

2–16. 17.

2–17. False

2–18. The third element in a list

2–19. Space

2–20. 17/4

2–21. 31 Audubon Terrace

2–22. 17 DIV 4

DECLARATION SECTION

An identifier is typed in the declaration section of a Pascal program. This section is physically located between the program heading and the program body. Diagramatically, a Pascal program is represented as follows:

Program heading

Declaration section

Program body

VAR

In the declaration section, identifiers are identified by type. This portion of the declaration section begins with the reserved word VAR. Following VAR, each identifier is listed; it is followed by a colon (:) and its type. For example,

```
VAR
   sales : REAL;
```

As you can see from this example, no punctuation follows the reserved word VAR, but a semicolon follows the actual declaration. If more than a single identifier is of a particular type, each must be defined.

```
VAR
   sales : REAL;
   profit : REAL;
```

When there are several identifiers of a particular type, they usually are not declared separately (as in the previous example). Rather, they are declared in the same statement, separated from one another by commas.

```
VAR
   sales, profit : REAL;
```

Again, for the sake of clarity, use comments generously. You may have to write the identifiers on separate lines to accommodate the comments.

```
VAR
   sales,          (* amount of sales *)
   profit          (* gross profit *)
     : REAL;
```

Sometimes, the type is located on the same line as the last identifier, as in the following example.

```
VAR
   sales,            (* amount of sales *)
   profit : REAL     (* gross profit *)
```

The VAR portion of the declaration section can be separated from the program heading and the program body (or other portions of the declaration section) by a line feed. This helps make the program more readable.

Constants

Another portion of the declaration section of a Pascal program is reserved for the specification of constants. As the name implies, constants are identifiers whose value will not change in the program.

This section begins with the reserved word CONST. The identifiers and their values are then listed. The identifier and its value are separated from one another by an equal sign (=). Following the value is a semicolon.

```
CONST
   Author = 'John E. Parnell';
   Pi = 3.14159;
```

Note that when a literal value is assigned to an identifier, it must be enclosed within single quotation marks ('). If the literal itself contains a single quotation mark, then two SINGLE quotation marks (not one double quotation mark) are used to signal the computer of the condition.

```
CONST
   WhoseCar = 'John''s';
```

Identifiers appearing in the CONST portion of the declaration section do not appear in the VAR portion. Only variables should appear in the VAR portion.

Procedures and Functions

Also located in the declaration section are PROCEDUREs and FUNC-TIONs. They are very similar in purpose, but quite different in operation. Both can be considered subroutines (that is, a set of statements that can be executed one or more times in one or more locations within a program). Subroutines are written only once, but accessed several times; this conserves computer memory.

In addition, procedures and functions allow you to isolate a section of the program to make development and debugging easier, since you need not be concerned with the other parts of the program. The formats for procedures and functions are similar, yet very different. The difference in format stems from their major functional difference: A function returns a value through its name, whereas a procedure may return no or many values.

Both procedures and functions are located in the declaration portion of a program, that is, after the program heading and before the BEGIN of the program body. Generally speaking, it is advisable to place procedures and functions after the VAR portion. Some implementations of Pascal even require this.

Just like a program in general, procedures and functions have a heading, declaration, and body sections. Since the format of procedures and functions are not identical, it is advisable to consider these two separately.

Procedures. When procedures are written, each should perform a single operation, not a series of unrelated ones. Procedures that are related to one another in a logical manner (for example, sorting names versus sorting zip codes) should be physically close to one another in the program.

When no parameters are to be passed between the procedure and the program, or vice versa, the procedure heading has the following format.

PROCEDURE ⟨identifier⟩;

If parameters are to be passed, then the following format is followed:

PROCEDURE ⟨identifier⟩ (⟨identifier(s)⟩ : ⟨type(s)⟩);

Note that in the latter format, the semicolon is not located after the name of the procedure. Rather, it is at the end of the heading, after the right parenthesis.

A third format is also possible. In this format, VAR is written inside the parentheses, before the first identifier.

PROCEDURE ⟨identifier⟩ (VAR ⟨identifier(s)⟩ : ⟨type(s)⟩);

The differences among these three formats are very important. We will consider them separately.

1. PROCEDURE ⟨identifier⟩;

This format is the most elementary of the three. This format is used when no parameters are to be passed between the program body and the procedure. Whatever occurs within the procedure does not affect the values of the parameters in the program body. Quite often, this type of procedure is used to write a stock output. For example, the following procedure causes the word *Page* to be written in the left-hand margin.

PROCEDURE Heading;

```
BEGIN (* Heading *)
   WRITELN ('Page')
END; (* Heading *)
```

To execute the previous procedure, place in the program body the following "procedure call."

Heading;

When the computer encounters this procedure call, it goes back to the declaration section of the program and finds the procedure called Heading. After executing the procedure, the computer returns to the first statement following the procedure call and continues the execution of the program body. The values of all parameters remain unchanged.

2. PROCEDURE ⟨identifier⟩ (⟨identifier(s)⟩ : ⟨type(s)⟩);

If parameters are to be passed to the procedure, then the previous format is used. Contained within the parentheses must be each parameter whose value is to be passed. Even though the parameters are typed in the calling body, they must be typed in the procedure heading. The variable types listed in this heading must agree with those of the main body.

The sequence of types in the procedure call must be identical to the sequence of types in the procedure heading. In the following example, the values of First and Second are passed to the procedure.

. . .

Trial (First, Second);

. . .

In this example, Trial is the name of the procedure. If First had been declared as CHAR in the main program body and Second as INTEGER, then the procedure heading should look like the following:

PROCEDURE Trial (First : CHAR, Second : INTEGER);

It should be noted that the specific identifier names from the main body need not be used in the procedure heading. Hence, the following is also a valid procedure for the above.

PROCEDURE Trial (One : CHAR; Two : INTEGER);

In this example of a procedure heading, One takes on the value of First, and Two takes on the value of Second.

When using procedures of this type (parameter passing), no matter what happens to the value of the identifiers listed in the heading, the values of the identifiers in the procedure call are not altered. Hence, First and Second retain their original values even if the values of One and Two change. If the same variable names were used in both the procedure call and in the procedure heading, the computer would keep track of the original values of the variables and then reassign these values to the identifiers when control returned to the program body.

3. PROCEDURE ⟨identifier⟩ (VAR ⟨identifier(s)⟩ : ⟨type(s)⟩);

Sometimes it is desirable to pass a value to a procedure and have this value change within the procedure. This new value is what is needed in the program body. To do this type of operation, the previous format is required.

Just like the second type procedure, the sequence of types of identifiers listed in the procedure call and procedure heading must be identical. Again, it is not necessary to use the same identifier names. In the following example, if the value passed to the procedure is a seven, the value returned is an eight.

PROCEDURE Add (VAR Number : INTEGER);

```
BEGIN (* Add *)
  NUMBER := Number + 1
END; (* Add *)
```

Suppose the procedure call was

    Add(First);

and the value of First going into this line was a seven. Then, in returning to the line after this one, First has the value of eight.

Functions. The Pascal language comes with 17 standard identifiers that are functions. These are as follows:

ABS	ARCTAN	CHR	COS
EOF	EOLN	EXP	LN
ODD	ORD	PRED	ROUND
SIN	SQR	SQRT	SUCC
TRUNC			

These are expanded on a bit more in the Appendix.

In addition to the standard functions, programmers can write their own functions. Like procedures, functions are located in the declaration section of a program after the VAR declarations and before the BEGIN of the main body. Unlike procedures, functions always represent a value. The format of a function call is as follows:

    ⟨identifier⟩;

When the computer encounters a function call, it immediately evaluates the function. The format of a function heading must be one or two of the following:

    FUNCTION ⟨identifier⟩ : ⟨type⟩;

or

    FUNCTION ⟨identifier⟩ ((⟨identifier(s)⟩ : ⟨type(s)⟩) : ⟨type⟩;

Within the function, the identifier name is assigned a value. The only place that this identifier can receive a value is through the function. In the following example, the function identifier Cube is given a value.

    FUNCTION Cube (Number : INTEGER) : INTEGER;

```
BEGIN (* Cube *)
  Cube := Number * Number * Number
END; (* Cube *)
```

Note the assignment statement in the function is for the identifier name. This was not the story in the case of a procedure.

In the previous example, the value Number was passed to the function and used therein. This was accomplished by the function call.

```
Cube(Number);
```

If the values are passed to the function, there must be a one-to-one correspondence between the arguments in the function call and the parameters in the function heading. The types of values passed must be identical to the order and number listed in the heading. Note that a function can be used to calculate only a single value, the value of the identifier name. Any other values are lost once the control is returned to the main program. Therefore, if more than one value is to be calculated, a procedure should be used.

The format of the function itself is virtually identical to that of a procedure. It has a declaration section as well as a main body contained within a BEGIN . . . END pair. The purpose and use of these two kinds of subprograms is very different.

NESTING

Following the heading of both a procedure and function is the declaration section. In this section are located all the items that can be located in the declaration section of the program itself. These include VAR, CONST, PROCEDURE, and FUNCTION. Identifiers located in this section exist only in this specific procedure or function. They have no value outside this specific procedure or function (or those declared therein, that is, nested). Since the nesting of procedures and functions is an important feature of Pascal, it should be considered at length. Since the methodology of nesting both procedures and functions is virtually identical, only the nesting of procedures is discussed here.

To nest procedures, you merely declare a procedure within the declaration section of a procedure. For example, in the following illustration, procedure Alpha is nested within procedure Beta.

```
PROCEDURE Beta;

   VAR
      . . .

   PROCEDURE Alpha;

   VAR
      . . .

   BEGIN (* Alpha *)
      . . .
   END; (* Alpha *)

BEGIN (* Beta *)
   . . .
END; (* Beta *)
```

In the previous example, whatever variables are declared in Beta are accessible by procedure Alpha. That is to say, they are "global" to the procedure. Whatever variables are declared within Alpha cannot be accessed by procedure Beta. They are "local" to procedure Alpha. Most computer systems allow for the nesting of up to six levels of procedures. Procedures that are nested within one procedure cannot be accessed by another, unrelated procedure.

EXERCISES

For exercises 2–23 through 2–33, consider the following sample program.

```
PROGRAM demo;
  VAR
    FirstVariable : INTEGER;
  PROCEDURE A;
    VAR
      SecondVariable : REAL;
    PROCEDURE B;
      VAR
        ThirdVariable : CHAR;
      BEGIN (* procedure B *)
```

```
        . . .
      END; (* procedure B *)
    BEGIN (* procedure A *)

      . . .
      B;

      . . .
    END; (* procedure A *)
    PROCEDURE C;
      VAR
        FourthVariable : INTEGER;
      PROCEDURE D;
        VAR
          FifthVariable : CHAR;
        BEGIN (* procedure D *)
          . . .
      END; (* procedure D *)
    PROCEDURE E;
      VAR
        SixthVariable : CHAR;
      BEGIN (* procedure E *)

        . . .
      END; (* procedure E *)
    BEGIN (* procedure C *)

      . . .
      D;

      . . .
      E;

      . . .
      E;

      . . .
    END; (* procedure C *)
  BEGIN (* demo *)

    . . .
    C;

    . . .
  END. (* demo *)
```

2–23. The variable declared in procedure D (FifthVariable) may be accessed in

a. all of program demo.

b. only procedures D and E.

c. only procedures D and A.

d. only procedure D.

e. only procedures A, B, and C.

2–24. The variable FirstVariable may be accessed in

a. all of program demo.

b. only procedures D and E.

c. only procedures D and A.

d. only procedures B and D.

e. only procedures A, B, and C.

2–25. SecondVariable may be accessed in

a. all of program demo.

b. only procedures D and E.

c. only procedures A and B.

d. only procedures A, B, and C.

e. only procedure A.

2–26. The variable ThirdVariable may be accessed in

a. all of program demo.

b. only in procedure B.

c. only in procedure A.

d. only in procedures A and B.

e. only in procedures C and E.

2–27. The variable declared in procedure E (SixthVariable) may be accessed in

a. only procedure E.

b. only procedure D.

c. all of program demo.

d. only in procedure C.

e. only in procedures A and B.

2–28. Variable FourthVariable may be accessed only in

a. procedure C.

b. procedure D.

    c. procedure E.

    d. procedures C and D.

    e. procedures C, D, and E.

2–29. Which of the following may be accessed by procedure D?

    a. FirstVariable only.

    b. FirstVariable and SecondVariable only.

    c. FourthVariable and FifthVariable only.

    d. FirstVariable, FourthVariable, and FifthVariable only.

    e. FirstVariable and Fifthvariable only.

2–30. Which of the following variables may be accessed by procedure B?

    a. ThirdVariable only.

    b. FirstVariable and ThirdVariable only.

    c. FirstVariable, SecondVariable, and ThirdVariable only.

    d. FourthVariable and FifthVariable only.

    e. every variable.

2–31. Procedure E is nested in procedure(s)

    a. A.

    b. B.

    c. C.

    d. D.

    e. C and D.

2–32. Which variable(s) are said to be global to the program?

    a. FirstVariable only.

    b. SecondVariable only.

    c. ThirdVariable only.

    d. FourthVariable only.

    e. FifthVariable and SixthVariable only

2–33. Assuming no GOTO statements in the entire program and no procedure or function calls other than those indicated, what is the sequence of procedures called?

    a. D, E, A, C

    b. C, D, E, E

   c. A, B, C, D

   d. D, B, C, A

   e. E, E, D, C

RECURSION

Another way of using procedures is recursion. Recursion involves having a procedure call itself. That is, within the procedure is a procedure call for itself. Here is an example of a recursive procedure.

```
PROCEDURE Increment (Number : INTEGER);

    BEGIN (* Increment *)
       Number := Number + 1;
       IF Number 100
          THEN Increment(Number);
       WRITELN (Number : 1)
    END; (* Increment *)
```

In this example, procedure Increment continues calling itself until the value of Number exceeds 100. Recursion is useful when there is a set of steps that must be repeatedly executed until a particular condition is met. The game "Towers of Hanoi" is an example of this process. Since this game is a common example of the use of recursion, a discussion of the game is warranted.

    The object of the game is to move a series of rings from one of three pegs to a second peg. The initial situation has the rings in an increasing order of size. When the game is completed, the rings are also to be in an increasing order of size. The following illustration shows the initial and final situations.

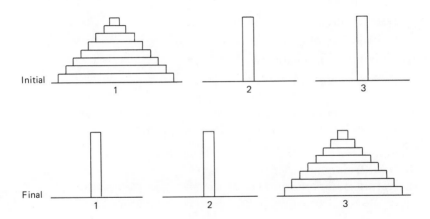

When the rings are moved, only one ring can be moved at a time. A larger ring cannot be placed on top of a smaller ring. The third peg is used as an intermediary for the movement from the initial peg to the final peg.

Moving the first two rings from peg 1 to peg 2 involves the following moves:

1. ring 1 from peg 1 to peg 3;
2. ring 2 from peg 1 to peg 2;
3. ring 1 from peg 3 to peg 2.

Moving ring 3 to peg 2 involves the following additional moves:

4. ring 3 from peg 1 to peg 3;
5. ring 1 from peg 2 to peg 1;
6. ring 2 from peg 2 to peg 3;
7. ring 1 from peg 1 to peg 2;
8. ring 2 from peg 3 to peg 1;
9. ring 1 from peg 2 to peg 1;
10. ring 3 from peg 3 to peg 2;
11. ring 1 from peg 1 to peg 3;
12. ring 2 from peg 1 to peg 2;
13. ring 1 from peg 3 to peg 2.

A closer examination of these moves should reveal a pattern of ring movements. This pattern would be programmed into a procedure, and this procedure would call itself as needed.

EXERCISES

2–34. The Fibonacci numbers are positive integers such that each number is the sum of the previous two. The first two numbers in the series are 1 and 1. The series looks like the following:

1 1 2 3 5 8 13 . . .

Therefore the Nth number is equal to the sum of the $(N - 1)$th and $(N - 2)$th numbers. Write a procedure in Pascal that determines the value of the Nth number in the series (a) by iteration and (b) by recursion. The value of N is passed to the procedure.

2–35. A factorial may be defined as a positive number that is equal to the product of that number and all its predecessors. For example, 5 factorial (written 5!) is equal to

5 * 4 * 3 * 2 * 1

or 120. Write a recursive procedure in Pascal to calculate N! The value of N is passed to the procedure.

2–36. To convert a number from base 10 to its binary equivalent, you must successively divide the number by two and take the remainder, if any. For example, to convert 69 to binary, the following divisions have to occur:

69 / 2 = 34 remainder 1

34 / 2 = 17 remainder 0

17 / 2 =   8 remainder 1

8 / 2   =   4 remainder 0

4 / 2   =   2 remainder 0

2 / 2   =   1 remainder 0

1 / 2   =   0 remainder 1

Hence, 69 in base 10 is equivalent to 1010001 in base 2. Write a recursive procedure in Pascal to convert the number N from base 10 to base 2. N is passed to the procedure.

2–37. Rewrite the procedure in exercise 2–36 to make the conversion to octal, that is, base 8. Again, N is passed to the procedure.

2–38. Rewrite the procedure in exercise 2–36 to make the conversion from base 10 to ANY base. Both N and the desired base are passed to the procedure.

2–39. To calculate the square root of a number by hand, you first separate the digits of the number into pairs, justifying at the decimal point. For example, the number 112345.67 is represented as:

11 23 45 . 67

Next, you determine what number, when squared, would not exceed the first pair from the left. In this example, that would be 3 (3 * 3 = 9, 9 < 11). This number is written above the pair. The square of this number is written below the pair. Hence, the calculation at this point appears as follows:

$$\begin{array}{r} 3 \\ \sqrt{11\ 23\ 45\ .\ 67} \\ 9 \end{array}$$

For the sake of the discussion, let's call the line where the 3 is located level 1, the line where the number whose square root is to be determined level 2, and the square of the level 1 number level 3.

The level 3 number is subtracted from the first pair of the level 2 number and the second level 2 pair is brought down to join the remainder on level 4.

```
Level 1      3
Level 2    √11 23 45 . 67
Level 3      9
Level 4      2 23
```

The number on level 1 is doubled, a zero is added, and it is divided into the level 4 number. The quotient is added to the divisor before the division occurs.

```
Level 1      3
Level 2    √11 23 45 . 67
Level 3      9
Level 4      2 23
Divisor 60
```

60 goes into 223 three times, hence the new divisor becomes 63.

```
Level 1      3
Level 2    √11 23 45 . 67
Level 3      9
Level 4      2 23
Divisor 63
```

The division occurs, and the remainder is written on level 6.

```
Level 1      3
Level 2    √11 23 45 . 67
```

Level 3	9
Level 4	2 23
Level 5	1 89
Level 6	34

The next pair from level 2 is brought down to level 6, and the process is continued until you both run out of level 2 numbers and the remainder of the division is 0. (If you run out of level 2 pairs before the remainder of the division is 0, pairs of zeros are brought down.) Another way of stopping the divisions is when the needed accuracy has been obtained in the level 1 number. The following shows the completion of this square root determination to eight decimal places of accuracy.

```
           3   3   5 . 1   8   0   0   5   6   0   8
        ┌─────────────────────────────────────────────
      √ │ 11  23  45 . 67  00  00  00  00  00  00  00

           9
          ───
           2  23

   63      1  89
          ──────
              34  45

  665       33  25
          ────────
               1  20  67

 6701          67  01
             ───────
               53  66  00

67028          53  62  24
             ───────────
                    3  76  00

670360                  0
                   ─────────
                    3  76  00  00
```

6703600	0
	3 76 00 00 00
67036005	3 35 18 00 25
	40 81 99 75 00
670360106	40 22 16 06 36
	59 83 68 64 00
6703601100	0
	59 83 68 64 00 00
67036011008	53 62 88 08 80 64
	6 20 80 55 19 36

Write the above recursive procedure in Pascal to have the computer calculate the square root of any positive number. The number, N, is passed to the procedure from the program body. The procedure should calculate the square root to a maximum of five decimal places.

THE PROGRAM BODY

Pascal Operators

The following is a listing of the Pascal operators used by most versions of Pascal.

Operator	Meaning
+	addition or set union
−	subtraction or set difference
*	multiplication or set intersection
/	division
DIV	integer division, that is, truncate remainder
MOD	modulus, that is, remainder of division

Operator	Meaning
AND	Boolean conjunction
OR	Boolean inclusive disjunction
NOT	Boolean negation
IN	test set membership
$\langle$	is less than
$\rangle$	is greater than
$\langle\,\rangle$	is not equal to
=	is equal to
$\langle =$	is less than or equal to
$\rangle =$	is greater than or equal to

Order of Precedence

First Order	NOT
Second Order	* / DIV MOD AND
Third Order	+ − OR
Fourth Order	$\langle =$ = $\rangle =$ $\langle\rangle$ $\langle$ $\rangle$ IN

NOTE:

1. Parentheses may alter these orders of precedence. When parentheses are used, the innermost set is evaluated first, followed by each outer set. Within sets of parentheses, the above order of precedence is followed.

2. Operators of equal precedence are executed in order, from left to right as listed within the statement.

Example:

$$4 + 2 / 2 + 3 - 7 * 2 \text{ DIV } 2$$

is evaluated in the following sequence of "steps."

$$1 -- 4 + \underline{2/2} + 3 - 7 * 2 \text{ DIV } 2$$

$$2 -- 4 + 1 + 3 - \underline{7 * 2} \text{ DIV } 2$$

$$3 -- 4 + 1 + 3 - \underline{14 \text{ DIV } 2}$$

4 -- 4 + 1 + 3 − 7

5 -- 5 + 3 − 7

6 -- 8 − 7

7 -- 1

The result of this computation is 1. Without rules for the order of precedence, the result would equal − 1, assuming that the execution proceeded from left to right as written.

Exercises

What is the result of each of the following computations?

2–40. 7 / 2 DIV 3
2–41. 4 * 3 + 2 − (7 + 3) MOD 3
2–42. 8 MOD (3 + 1)
2–43. 7 DIV 2
2–44. 1 * 4 / 2 * 3 + 1
2–45. (5 / 9)*(98.6 − 32)
2–46. 37 * 9 / 5 + 32
2–47. 17 DIV 4 MOD 3
2–48. 4 + 2 * 3 / 4
2–49. 9 − 3 * 2 − (2 + 1) * 2

Results of Operations

Operation	Result
real + real	real
real + integer	real
integer + real	real
integer + integer	integer
real − real	real
real − integer	real
integer − real	real
integer − integer	integer
real * real	real

Operation	Result
real * integer	real
integer * real	real
integer * integer	integer
real / real	real
real / integer	real
integer / real	real
integer / integer	integer
real MOD real	error
real MOD integer	error
integer MOD real	error
integer MOD integer	integer
real DIV real	error
real DIV integer	error
integer DIV real	error
integer DIV integer	integer

Exercises

Assume that the following declarations have been made.

```
VAR
    first, second, third, temp1 : REAL;
    fourth, fifth, sixth, temp2   : INTEGER;
```

If the indicated assignments are made, what is the output for the following program segments? Indicate errors, if present.

```
      first := 1;
    second := 2;
      third := 3;
    fourth := 4;
      fifth := 5;
      sixth := 6;
```

2–50. templ := first * second / first + third * fourth;
        WRITELN (templ);

2–51. temp2 := sixth + fifth + fourth + third;
      WRITELN (temp2);

2–52. temp1 := first + second + sixth MOD fourth;
      WRITELN (temp1);

2–53. temp2 := (second + third) DIV fifth;
      WRITELN (temp2);

2–54. temp1 := fourth – fifth;
      WRITELN (temp1);

Standard Pascal Functions

Function Format	Parameter Type(s)	Resulting Type(s)	Returns
	Integer	Integer	
ABS(parameter)			absolute value of the parameter
	Real	Real	
	Integer	Integer	
ARCTAN(parameter)			arctangent of the parameter in radians
	Real	Real	
CHR(parameter)	Integer	CHAR	character whose ASCII value is specified
	Integer	Real	
COS(parameter)			cosine of the parameter, which must be in radians
	Real	Real	
EOF(file)	File	Boolean	end-of-file test
EOLN(file)	File	Boolean	end-of-line test
	Integer	Real	
EXP(parameter)			e to the parameter power
	Real	Real	
	Integer	Real	

Function Format	Parameter Type(s)	Resulting Type(s)	Returns
LN(parameter)			natural logarithm of the parameter
	Real	Real	
ODD(parameter)	Integer	Boolean	odd test
ORD(parameter)	Ordinal	Integer	ordinal number of parameter
PRED(parameter)	Ordinal	Same	unique predecessor of parameter
ROUND(parameter)	Real	Integer	parameter rounded to the nearest integer
	Integer	Real	
SIN(parameter)			sin of the parameter which must be in radians
	Real	Real	
	Integer	Real	
SQR(parameter)			raises the parameter to the second power
	Real	Real	
	Integer	Real	
SQRT(parameter)			square root of the parameter
	Real	Real	
SUCC(parameter)	Ordinal	Same	unique successor of the parameter
TRUNC(parameter)	Real	Integer	truncate the decimal portion of the parameter

Exercises

Given the following declarations, indicate the necessary type of the variable called Temp so as not to generate an error. If there is an error, indicate what it is, as well as how to correct it.

```
VAR
  FirstParameter := REAL;
  SecondParameter := INTEGER;
  ThirdParameter := CHAR;
```

2–55. Temp := ABS(ThirdParameter);

2–56. Temp := CHR(FirstParameter);

2–57. Temp := EOF)SecondParameter);

2–58. Temp := EXP(FirstParameter);

2–59. Temp := ODD(FirstParameter);

2–60. Temp := PRED(ThirdParameter);

2–61. Temp := SIN(SecondParameter);

2–62. Temp := SQRT(FirstParameter);

2–63. Temp := TRUNC(SecondParameter);

2–64. Temp := ARCTAN(ThirdParameter);

2–65. Temp := COS(FirstParameter);

2–66. Temp := EOLN(FirstParameter);

2–67. Temp := LN(FirstParameter);

2–68. Temp := ORD(ThirdParameter);

2–69. Temp := ROUND(FirstParameter);

2–70. Temp := SQR(SecondParameter);

2–71. Temp := SUCC(ThirdParameter);

Assignment Statement

General Form.

```
parameter := value;
```

The parameter may be any valid variable. The type used must correspond to the type of the value specified. If the two types do not coincide, then an error is generated.

Examples:

```
Temporary := 17;
Age := Today − Birthdate;
Counter := Counter + 1;
Name := 'JOHN';
```

Expressions. An expression (that is, a formula) may be used in an assignment statement. The expression must be located to the right of the assignment operator. Only a single operand may be located to the left of the assignment operator.

Valid assignments:

    Product := 4 * 7;
    Balance := Balance + Deposit;
    Balance := Balance − Withdrawal;
    MyInheritance := TotalInheritance / NumberOfHeirs;

Invalid assignments:

    Month * DaysInMonth := DaysSoFar;
    'PARNELL' := Name;

In order to use an expression, the value of each parameter must be specified before it is used in the expression. In Pascal, unlike some other languages, a parameter is not assigned a value of zero or a null prior to its first use.

Exercises

Translate the following into valid Pascal assignment statements.

2–72. The square root of the sum of A squared and B squared.

2–73. Increment J by 2.

2–74. P = T * (1 + X / T)^200

2–75. Y = (M) * (X) + B

2–76. E = (M) * (C^2)

2–77. CelsiusTemperature = (5 / 9) * (FahrenheitTemperature − 32)

2–78. HeatLost = Mass * ChangeInTemperature * SpecificHeat

2–79. Author = John E. Parnell

2–80. Decrement P by 100.

2–81. $P1 = \dfrac{V2 * P2 * (T1 + 273)}{(T2 + 273) * V2}$

Simple Conditional Statements

The IF . . . THEN statement has the following format.

    IF ⟨condition⟩
    THEN ⟨statement⟩

Following the reserved word IF is the condition that is tested. If the condition is valid (Boolean TRUE), then the statement following the reserved word THEN is executed. In the following example, if the value of

A is greater than the value of B, then the words *A is greater than B.* will be written to the file.

```
IF A ) B
THEN WRITELN ('A is greater than B.');
```

Multiple Simple Conditional Statements. It is possible to have more than a single condition that must be met for the statement to be executed. When more than one condition is present, each must be separated from the other by a Boolean operator such as AND or OR. Since the Boolean operators have a very high order of precedence, each of the conditions in a multi-condition IF . . . THEN statement should be enclosed within parentheses. For example,

```
IF (A ) B) AND (A ) C)
THEN WRITELN ('A is the largest number.');
```

In multi-condition IF . . . THEN statements, all conditions must be TRUE before the statement following the THEN is executed if the BOO-LEAN operator is AND. However, if the operator is OR, then if either condition is TRUE, the statement is executed. In the following example, if either B is greater than A or C is greater than A, the sentence *A is not the largest number.* will be output.

```
IF (B ) A) OR (C ) A)
THEN WRITELN ('A is not the largest number.');
```

Multiple Executions in Simple Conditional Statements. In order for more than one statement to be executed following the reserved word THEN, the statements must be enclosed within a BEGIN . . . END pair. For example, the following program segment writes the words *Today is Monday* to the file.

```
Today : = 'Monday';
IF Today = 'Monday'
THEN WRITE ('Today is ');
     WRITELN (Today);
```

However, in the following example, the sentence is written only when the condition is valid.

```
Today : = 'Monday';
IF Today = 'Monday'
```

```
THEN
  BEGIN
    WRITE ('Today is ');
    WRITELN (Today)
  END;
```

In the former example, if the assignment statement was changed to

```
Today := 'Tuesday';
```

then only *Tuesday* would be written to the file. This is because the statement

```
WRITELN (Today);
```

would not be considered a part of the conditional response. Therefore, it would be executed regardless of whether the condition were TRUE or FALSE.

Following the THEN could be any valid statement(s). For example, the following would cause a countdown from 10 to 1, followed by the word *BLASTOFF* being written to the file.

```
IF Count = 10
THEN
  BEGIN
    FOR Shuttle := 10 DOWNTO 1 DO
      WRITELN (Shuttle : 1);
    WRITELN ('BLASTOFF')
  END;
```

Complex Conditional Statements

IF . . . THEN statements may be extended. This extension allows for the execution of one statement(s) if one set of conditions is satisfied and a second statement(s) if the set is not satisfied. The following example assumes a 24-hour clock.

```
IF Time ⟨ 12
THEN WRITELN ('It is morning.')
ELSE WRITELN ('It is afternoon.');
```

The ELSE statement, that is, the statement(s) following the ELSE, is executed whenever the condition following the IF is FALSE.

The Boolean operator AND in the IF portion of the conditional means that whenever *either* of the conditions is FALSE, the statement(s) following the ELSE is executed. The OR operator means that whenever neither condition is valid, the ELSE statement(s) is executed.

Any valid Pascal statement can follow the word ELSE, including another IF . . . THEN(. . . ELSE) statement. The following is a valid Pascal statement:

```
IF time ⟨ 12
THEN WRITELN ('It is morning.')
ELSE
    IF time ⟨ 17
    THEN WRITELN ('It is afternoon.')
    ELSE WRITELN ('It is evening.');
```

Note that in the previous example, if time equals 10, then the words *It is morning.* are written (not *It is afternoon.*) The reason for this is that as soon as the THEN is executed, the computer skips to the end of the statement, as signified by the location of the semicolon (;). In addition, no semicolon should be placed after any but the last THEN (or ELSE) statement. Placing a semicolon before this causes the computer to use that statement as the end of the IF . . . THEN(. . . ELSE) statement and then report an error because the next statement is not complete. For example, the following is an invalid statement:

```
IF time ⟨ 12
THEN WRITELN ('It is morning.');
ELSE
    IF time ⟨ 17
THEN WRITELN ('It is afternoon.');
ELSE WRITELN ('It is evening.');
```

The computer would regard the first two lines as one complete statement. An error would then be generated because a valid Pascal statement cannot begin with the word ELSE.

Just as there can be in a simple IF . . . THEN statement, in an IF . . . THEN(. . . ELSE) statement, there can be multiple conditionals and multiple execution statements. The multiple conditions must be separated by Boolean operators. The multiple execution statements can follow either the THEN or the ELSE, or both. These statements must also be enclosed within a BEGIN . . . END pair. When using the BEGIN . . . END pair, do not follow the END with a semicolon unless it is at the very end of the entire IF . . . THEN(. . . ELSE) statement.

Nesting Conditional Statements

If the statement following the THEN or ELSE portion of the conditional statement is another IF . . . THEN(. . . ELSE) conditional statement, then you have created a nested conditional statement. Extra care must be taken in the use of nesting. Most Pascal compilers allow only a maximum of six levels of nesting. More than this is either ignored or generates an error, depending on the compiler. Most programmers feel that when a program is written with that many levels of nesting, it is too easy to make an error. There has to be a better way of writing the program.

Another problem that occurs when using nesting is that it is relatively easy to lose track of which ELSE goes with which THEN. Remember, indentation does not remedy the situation. Examine the following program segment.

```
IF Time < 12
THEN
  IF Today = 'Monday'
  THEN WRITELN ('Hi')
ELSE WRITELN ('There');
```

The indentation suggests that the ELSE statement goes with the first THEN statement. However, the computer has been programmed to match an ELSE statement with the most recent unmatched THEN statement. Hence, the ELSE statement is coupled with the second THEN statement, and not the first. This confusion is very common among beginning programmers.

Consider the following program segment:

```
IF (Today = 'Monday') OR (Today = 'Wednesday')
THEN WRITELN ('Carol is on duty.')
ELSE
  IF (Today = 'Tuesday') OR (Today = 'Thursday')
  THEN WRITELN ('John is in charge.')
ELSE
  IF (Today = 'Friday')
  THEN WRITELN ('Carl is on duty.');
```

CASE STATEMENTS

The previous program segment is an example of nested IF . . . THEN(. . . ELSE) statements. This could be replaced by a single CASE statement. The general format of a CASE statement is:

```
CASE ⟨case selector⟩ OF
    ⟨case label list⟩ : ⟨case execution statement⟩
END;
```

An equivalent CASE statement for the former program segment is the following:

```
CASE Today OF
    'Monday', 'Wednesday' : WRITELN ('Carol is on duty.');
    'Tuesday', 'Thursday'  : WRITELN ('John is in charge.');
    'Friday'               : WRITELN ('Carl is on duty.')
END;
```

In this program segment, as in the former, Carol is on duty on Monday and Wednesday. It's John on Tuesday and Thursday, and Carl is on duty on Friday. If it's Saturday or Sunday, then none of the above is written. What happens if the value of the case selector is not in the case selection list depends on the compiler used. Possible outcomes may range from a run-time error to just the execution of the next statement in the program. Check your specific compiler before using the CASE statement.

Note that if the case label list is a literal, then it must be enclosed within single quotation marks. If the case label list is to be a numerical quantity, then the list is not enclosed within quotation marks. When there is more than a single item for the label list line, the items are separated by commas. Unlike acceptable rules of English, in Pascal, the comma must be outside the quotation marks, lest it be considered a part of the literal. Also note that each member of the case label list, except for the last, is to be terminated by a semicolon.

With CASE statements, an error is generated if the case selector is not of the same type as the case label list. In the previous program segment, Today would have to be declared as type PACKED ARRAY. The one type that cannot be used for the case selector is REAL.

In the CASE statement, as with the IF . . . THEN(. . . ELSE) statement, it is possible to have multiple statements executed for a particular label. If this is to be the case, then the CASE execution statements would start with BEGIN and terminate with END. Within the BEGIN . . . END pair would be located the multiple statements. An example of this type of CASE statement follows:

```
CASE Today OF
    'Monday', 'Wednesday' : WRITELN ('Carol is on duty.');
    'Tuesday', 'Thursday'  : WRITELN ('John is in charge.');
    'Friday'               : WRITELN ('Carl is on duty.');
```

```
'Saturday', 'Sunday'      : BEGIN
                            WRITELN ('Consultants are on duty');
                            WRITELN ('only Monday-Friday.')
                          END
  END;
```

FOR LOOPS

Another method of controlling the execution of a statement is through the use of a FOR loop. The format for this type of loop is:

```
FOR ⟨numeric variable⟩ := ⟨first value⟩ TO ⟨last value⟩ DO
    ⟨statement⟩;
```

The numeric variable must be so declared to avoid an error. The beginning value can be explicitly stated or can be a numeric variable itself. The same holds true for the ending value. The beginning value must be less than the ending value for the loop to be executed. The statement following the reserved word DO may be any valid Pascal statement, including another FOR loop.

In executing a FOR loop, the computer first assigns the beginning value to the numeric variable. It then executes the statement that follows DO. The numeric variable's value is incremented by one and its value is compared with the ending value. If it is less, then the statement following DO is again executed. This cycle of increment-compare-execute is repeated until the value of the numeric variable exceeds the stated ending value. At that point, the program passes on to the statement after the one following DO. In the following example, the numbers 1 through 10 are written:

```
FOR Counter := 1 to 10 DO
    WRITELN (Counter:1);
```

Regardless of whether the FOR loop is an incremental or decremental loop, unless it is told otherwise, the computer executes only a single statement following the DO. To signify that more than one statement is to be executed, use the BEGIN . . . END pair. In the following example, the characters *T-minus*, followed by the number, are written each time:

```
FOR Counter := 10 DOWNTO 1 DO
    BEGIN
```

```
      WRITE ('T-minus ');
      WRITELN (Counter:1)
   END;
```

Even though the indentation might suggest otherwise, the following example does not produce the same output as the preceding example does.

```
   FOR Counter := 10 DOWNTO 1 DO
      WRITE ('T-minus ');
      WRITELN (Counter:1);
```

The FOR loop is appropriate to use when a statement or set of statements are to be executed a specified number of times. On occasion, however, it is desirous that there be an execution only when a specific set of conditions is valid—something like combining a FOR loop with an IF . . . THEN(. . . ELSE). There are actually two ways of doing this: the REPEAT and WHILE loops.

REPEAT LOOPS

In a REPEAT loop, the format is:

```
   REPEAT
      ⟨statement⟩;
      ⟨statement⟩;
      . . .
      ⟨statement⟩

   UNTIL ⟨condition⟩;
```

In this type of loop, the statements between the words REPEAT and UNTIL are executed for as long as the condition is valid. An example follows:

```
   REPEAT
      WRITELN (Counter:1);
      Counter := Counter + 1
   UNTIL Counter 10;
```

In this example, the value of Counter is written out until it reaches a value of 10.

In executing a REPEAT loop, the computer tests for the validity of the condition *after* executing the enclosed statement(s) once. In the previous example, if the initial value of Counter is 10, then 10 is output and Counter is incremented to 11, at which point the loop ends. If, however, the initial value is 11, then 11 is output and Counter incremented to 12 before the validity check. The difference here might be very important. The type of loop wherein the validity is checked *before* execution of the enclosed statement(s) is a WHILE loop.

WHILE LOOPS

The format of a WHILE loop is:

```
WHILE ⟨condition⟩ DO
  BEGIN
    ⟨statement⟩;
    ⟨statement⟩;
    . . .
    ⟨statement⟩
  END;
```

If the previous example had been written using a WHILE loop, it might have looked like the following:

```
WHILE Counter ⟨ 11 DO
  BEGIN
    WRITELN (Counter:1);
    Counter := Counter + 1
  END;
```

In this example, if Counter equals 10 initially, then the number 10 is output, followed by an increment to 11. On the other hand, if Counter equals 11 initially, then nothing is output by this program segment. In other words, in a WHILE loop, the condition's validity is checked *before* the execution of the statement(s) enclosed between BEGIN and END. This differs from the REPEAT loop.

Both REPEAT and WHILE statements have their place in computer programs. But because of how they are executed by the computer, care must be taken when selecting the proper one to use in a program.

EXERCISES

What is the output for each of the following program segments (2–82 through 2–87)?

2–72. Sum := 0;
       FOR Counter := 1 TO 10 DO
          Sum := Sum + 1;
       WRITELN (Sum:10)

2–73. Sum := 0;
       FOR Counter1 := 1 TO 10 DO
          BEGIN
             FOR Counter2 := 100 DOWNTO 1 DO
                Sum := Sum + 1
          END;
       WRITELN (Sum:10)

2–74. Sum := 0;
       WHILE Sum ⟨ 100 DO
          Sum := Sum + 1;
       WRITELN (Sum:10)

2–75. While Sum ⟨ 100 DO
          BEGIN
             Sum := 0;
             Sum := Sum + 1
          END;
       WRITELN (Sum:10)

2–76. Sum := 0;
       REPEAT
          Sum := Sum + 1
       UNTIL Sum = 100;
       WRITELN (Sum:10)

2–77. Sum := 0;
       REPEAT
          Sum := Sum + 1;
          WRITELN (Sum:10)
       UNTIL Sum = 100;
       WRITELN (Sum:10)

2–78. Your company has just purchased a large number of computer clocks at a very good price. Unfortunately, they give the time in a 24-hour format (1:35 P.M. comes up as 13:35). Write a statement in Pascal to convert a time given in a 24-hour format to an A.M.-

P.M. format. Assume that the time for the 24-hour clock is in the form of two integers, hours and minutes.

2–79. Write a CASE statement to output the number of days in a month, given the first three characters of the name of the month. Assume that you are dealing with a non-leap year.

2–80. Rewrite the statement in exercise 2–89, allowing for the possibility of leap years.

2–81. Using a FOR loop, write a program segment to output the amount of interest paid annually on an Individual Retirement Account (IRA). Since the interest rate may vary from a guaranteed minimum of 5 percent to the current 15 percent, your program segment should calculate the yield for each level between these figures, in increments of 0.1 percent.

2–82. Rewrite the program segment in exercise 2–91 using a WHILE loop.

2–83. Rewrite the program segment in exercise 2–91 using a REPEAT loop.

2–84. Many computers cannot store as an INTEGER value a number greater than 32,767. Write a WHILE loop to determine which power of two this value is one less than.

2–85. Write a program segment to determine the maximum real number that a computer can represent. (Since this number is usually very large, do not have the computer output every number until this maximum is reached. It'll take too long!) An endless loop will have to be employed.

2–86. Given that the first day of a month falls on a Tuesday, write a Pascal program to determine which day of the week each of the following dates fall on: 5, 15, 25, 28.

2–87. You have been asked to pair up partners for a dinner party. The names of the men are on one list; the names of the women are on another. Whoever set up the lists made a mistake. They made up the list of men with the shortest man at the top of the list and the tallest at the bottom, with everybody else in order by height. The list of women is in reverse order, that is, tallest to shortest. Each list contains 50 names. Write a program segment to match up people of similar heights, taking one from each list. The men's names are stored in an array called man and the women's names are stored in one called woman.

3

Data Types and Structures

PRIMITIVE DATA TYPES

Integer Numbers

Numbers can be expressed in one of two forms—integer or real. Integer values can be either positive or negative. These numbers have no decimal portion; they are only whole numbers. The maximum integer value for many computer systems is 32767; the minimum is -32768. The reason for this stems from how integers are stored in a computer. All values in a computer are represented by a series of zeros and ones. This is called the binary system. The zeros and ones are called *binary digits*, or *bits* for short. In the binary system, only these bits are used—no 2s, 3s, or any other numbers. The first 10 binary numbers and their base 10 equivalent are as follows.

Binary Number	Base 10 Number
0	1
10	2
11	3
100	4
101	5
110	6
111	7
1000	8
1001	9
1010	10

A 16-bit computer uses all 16 bits, save one, to make up an integer. Using a maximum of 15 bits, then, the largest number possible is

111111111111111 = 32,767

The sixteenth bit, the leftmost bit, is reserved as the sign bit. When it is zero, the number is positive, when it is one, the number is negative. Hence, the largest integer number should actually be represented as

0111111111111111

Adding one to this number causes an overflow into the sign column.

At times, numbers greater than this maximum (sometimes referred to as MAXINT, for MAXimum INTeger) are required. When this happens, you must use real numbers. Generally, the largest real number is $10**38$, the smallest $10**-38$ (for most small computers). Real numbers can be either positive or negative. They can also have a decimal portion. Real numbers are written in a manner that most of us are unfamiliar with. Small real numbers are written in a regular fashion—for example, 3.7 and −14.9. However, very large or very small real numbers are written using floating-point notation. This is sometimes also referred to as scientific or exponential notation.

Floating-Point Numbers

Floating-point notation involves the use of the character E. The E is not an alphabetic character in this case, but rather means a power of 10. The number that follows the E is the power to which 10 is raised. The following illustrates how the E is used.

Real Number	Base 10 Equivalent
4E + 02	400
3.7E − 02	0.037
− 14E + 01	− 140
6.9E + 10	69000000000

When writing large real numbers and integers, do not use a comma. For example, 32,767 is written as 32767; 15 million is written as 15000000, not 15,000,000.

CHAR

A second type of primitive data is CHAR. This type of data cannot have mathematical operations performed on it. Examples of this symbolic data are a person's name, a street address, and a zip code. In some languages, this type of data is sometimes referred to as literal or string data. In Pascal, a single character may be assigned to a variable of type CHAR. More than one character requires an array, and in particular, a PACKED ARRAY. Packed arrays are discussed later in this chapter.

BOOLEAN

The last type of primitive data is BOOLEAN. This type of data may have a value of only TRUE or FALSE. It is a type of logic data. Variables that are declared to be type BOOLEAN cannot take on numerical or character values. Most often, this type of data is used in conditional statements.

ARRAYS

The previous discussion involved data types that were unrelated to one another (at least, judging from their names, they seem to be unrelated). At times, the relationship between variables is difficult to determine. For example, variables X and Y can both be declared INTEGER, yet they may or may not be related.

An array is a data type, the members of which all share the same type, are referred to by the same name, and are related to one another. An example of an array follows:

```
Number = ARRAY [1 .. 10] OF INTEGER;
```

In this declaration, the identifier Number is the name of the array. It is composed of integers. The various elements of the array have a subscript that ranges from 1 to 10. In this example, it is possible to show the relationship between the numbers of the array.

```
Number[1]
Number[2]
...
Number[10]
```

Each member of the array can be accessed by the use of a variable to represent its subscript. In the following program segment, the value for each member of the array is taken from the keyboard.

```
...
FOR Counter := 1 TO 10 DO
   READ (Number[Counter]);
...
```

This is a lot easier than the following:

```
...
READ (Number[1], Number[2], ..., Number[10]);
...
```

In the previous examples, note how the subscript was contained within square brackets, [ ]. Parentheses will not work. The square brackets must be butted up next to the variable.

Also note that the subscript can be a variable. This is true when the array is used (as the former example shows), and also when the array is declared, as the following example shows:

```
Number = ARRAY [Beginning ... Ending] OF INTEGER;
```

In this example, the identifiers Beginning and Ending must also be defined. The beginning and ending values in the range are separated by two periods. There is no space between these periods. The periods may abut the two values, or they may be separated from the values by a space. The values may be any ordinal type, that is, any type but REAL. Further examples of arrays follow.

```
Letter = ARRAY [1 .. 26] OF CHAR;

Value = ARRAY [−7 .. 14] OF INTEGER;
```

In the former example, the identifier Letter may be accessed by any subscript between 1 and 26, whereas in the latter case, the subscript varies from −7 to 14.

Arrays are declared in the TYPE portion of the declaration section, not the VAR section. In the following example, the first declaration is proper, but the second is not.

```
TYPE
  Number = ARRAY [1 .. 10] OF INTEGER;

VAR
  Number = ARRAY [1 .. 10] OF INTEGER;
```

To declare an array in the VAR section, you must first declare it in the TYPE section. The following shows how this is done:

```
TYPE
  A = ARRAY [1 .. 10] OF INTEGER;

VAR
  Number : A;
```

An advantage of doing this is that many variables can share a single TYPE.

```
TYPE
  A = ARRAY [1 .. 10] OF INTEGER;

VAR
  Number : A;
  Age : A;
  Course : A;
```

There is less typing involved with the above method. For many people, less typing may mean fewer typographical errors.

MULTIDIMENSIONAL ARRAYS

So far, only one-dimensional arrays have been considered. In Pascal, it is possible to have arrays of arrays, that is, multidimensional arrays. To declare an array of arrays, you might use the following format:

```
Number = ARRAY [1 .. 10] OF ARRAY [1 .. 10] OF INTEGER;
```

This declares a 10-by-10 two-dimensional array. Another way of declaring this array is as follows:

```
Number = ARRAY [1 .. 10, 1 .. 10] OF INTEGER;
```

In a two-dimensional array, the two dimensions need not be the same size.

```
Number = ARRAY [1 .. 10, −7 .. 14] OF INTEGER;
```

The members of the previous array could be shown as follows:

```
Number[1, − 7]  Number[1, − 6]  ...  Number[1,14]
Number[2, − 7]  Number[2, − 6]  ...  Number[2,14]
```

...
Number[10, − 7] Number[10, − 6]   ...   Number[10,14]

As you can see from the prevous illustration, the general format of
the two-dimensional array is Number[A,B], where A ranges in value from
1 to 10, and B ranges in value from − 7 to 14. Just as can be done in the
one-dimensional array, in a two-dimensional array, variables can be sub-
stituted for the beginning and ending values in the range, both in its
declaration and in its usage.

...

```
TYPE
  Number = ARRAY [A .. B, C .. D] OF INTEGER;
```

...
```
FOR Fcounter := A TO B DO
  FOR Scounter := C TO D DO
    READ (Number[Fcounter,Scounter]);
```
...
In Pascal, arrays need not be limited to two dimensions. Virtually
any size that a computer's memory can handle can be declared. This is
also a drawback of arrays. Unlike files, the size of an array, regardless of
how many dimensions it has, is limited by the amount of computer memory. Large arrays cannot fit into small memory space.

PACKED ARRAYS

One way of utilizing more of the computer's memory space is by packing
an array. This is done by using the reserved word PACKED in the declaration of the array. An example of this is as follows:

```
Number = PACKED ARRAY [1 .. 10] OF INTEGER;
```

In packing an array, space that is not used is freed up for other uses.
Suppose the unpacked array looks like this:

```
.........1
.........2
.........3
.........4
.........5
```

```
.........6
.........7
.........8
.........9
........10
```

When the array is packed, it takes on the following appearance:

```
....1....2
....3....4
....5....6
....7....8
....9...10
```

Even though an array is declared as PACKED, the computer is still able to keep track of all the elements. What, then, is wrong with using packed arrays all the time? The answer is time. It takes the computer more time to access a packed array than an unpacked array. The programmer must decide if the tradeoff is worthwhile.

EXERCISES

3–1. Which of the following statements, when used in the TYPE declaration section of a program, produces an error?

    a. Suit = (Club, Spade, Diamond, Heart);
       Deck = ARRAY [1 .. 13] OF Suit;
    b. Men = (George, Harry, Paul);
       HoursWorked = ARRAY [George .. Paul] OF 0 ..40;
    c. Screen = PACKED ARRAY [1 .. 80, 1 .. 24] OF CHAR;
    d. Grades = PACKED ARRAY [1 .. 10] OF 0% .. 100%
    e. Day = (Sunday, Monday, Tuesday, Wednesday, Thursday, Friday, Saturday);
       Month = ARRAY [1 .. 31] OF Day

3–2. If a company has 15 employees, each of whom has a different salary, which of the following is the best TYPE definition for keeping their records?

    a. Wage : 0 .. 10000;
       Salary : PACKED ARRAY [1 .. 15] OF Wage;
    b. Wage : 0 .. 10000;
       Salary : ARRAY [Wage] of 1 .. 15;

        c. Salary : ARRAY [1 .. 15] OF 1 .. 15;

        d. Salary : ARRAY [0 .. 10000] OF 1 .. 15;

        e. Salary = ARRAY [1 .. 15] OF 0 .. 10000;

3–3. A computer store needs to keep track of each of its different computers and their prices. Which of the following TYPE definitions is best suited to the needs of the store?

        a. Computers = (Apple, Osborne, IBM, Kaypro, Heathkit);
           Prices = ARRAY [Computers] OF REAL;

        b. Computers = (Apple, Osborne, IBM, Kaypro, Heathkit);
           Prices = ARRAY [Computers] OF INTEGER;

        c. PriceRange = 0.00 .. 10000.00;
           Computers = (Apple, Osborne, IBM, Kaypro, Heathkit);
           Prices = ARRAY [Computers] OF PriceRange;

        d. PriceRange = 0.00 .. 10000.00;
           Computers = (Apple, Osborne, IBM, Kaypro, Heathkit);
           Prices = ARRAY [PriceRange] OF Computers;

        e. Prices : PACKED ARRAY [Apple, Osborne, IBM, Kaypro, Heathkit] OF REAL;

3–4. Which of the following TYPE definitions is an equivalent definition of Decks, given the first three definitions?
Suit = (Hearts, Spades, Clubs, Diamonds);
Card = (Ace, Two, Three, Four, Five, Six, Seven, Eight, Nine, Ten, Jack, Queen, King);
Player = (Jack, Jill, Bill, Kevin);
Decks = ARRAY [1 .. 2] of ARRAY [Suit] OF ARRAY [Card] OF Player;

        a. Decks = ARRAY [1 .. 2, Suit, Card, Player] OF INTEGER;

        b. Decks = ARRAY [Suit, Card, Player] OF 1 .. 2;

        c. Decks = PACKED ARRAY [1 .. 2, Suit, Card, Player];

        d. Decks = PACKED ARRAY [1 .. 2, Suit] OF
           ARRAY [Card] OF ARRAY [Player];

        e. Decks = ARRAY [1 .. 2, Hearts .. Diamonds, Card] OF Player;

Exercises 3–5 through 3–7 deal with the following TYPE definitions:

        Employees = (Mike, Joe, Joseph, Kevin, John);

        Salary = REAL;

        Tax = ARRAY [Mike .. John] OF REAL;

3–5. For what condition are the above definitions most useful?

a. All the employees get the same salary, but have different taxes.
b. All the employees get the same salary and the same taxes.
c. The employees get different salaries and taxes.
d. The employees get different salaries but the same taxes.
e. The employees get different salaries and there are no taxes.

3–6. If a procedure definition is of the form

```
PROCEDURE PrintNetSalaries (Taxes : Tax; Gross : Salary);

VAR
   Loop : Employees;

BEGIN (* PrintNetSalaries *)
   FOR Loop := ...

      ...

      ...
END; (* PrintNetSalaries *)
```

which of the following Pascal statements is best suited?

a. WRITELN ('The net salary for ', Loop, 'is ', Gross − Taxes[Loop]);
b. WRITELN ('The net salary is ', Gross − Taxes(Loop));
c. WRITELN ('The net salary is ', Gross − Taxes[Tax]);
d. WRITELN ('The net salary is ', Gross − Tax[Loop]);
e. WRITELN ('The net salary is ', Gross − Taxes[Loop]);

3–7. Which of the following VAR definitions would be most useful?

a. Loop = Employees;
   Taxes = Tax;
   Gross = Salary;
b. Loop : Employees;
   Gross : Salary − Tax[Loop];
c. Gross : Salary;
   Taxes : Tax;
   Loop : Employees;
d. Taxes : Tax[Employees];
   Gross : Salary;
e. Gross : Salary[Employees] OF Tax;

3–8. Given the global TYPE and VAR definitions

```
TYPE
   Car = (Ford, GM, Honda);
   Options = (DualMirrors, PowerBrakes, ElectricWindows);
```

```
VAR
    Price = ARRAY [Car] OF ARRAY [Options] OF REAL;
```

which of the following will *not* cause an error in the body of the PASCAL program?

a. WRITELN ('The price of the option is ',Price[Car][Option]);
b. WRITELN ('The price of power brakes on a Ford is ', Price[Car][Options]);
c. WRITELN ('The price of dual mirrors on a GM is ', Price[Car][Options]);
d. WRITELN ('The price of electric windows in a Honda is ', Price[Honda][ElectricWindows];
e. WRITELN ('The price of dual mirrors on a Ford is ', Car[Price][DualMirrors];

3–9. Which of the following applications is best suited to arrays?

a. The storage of the names of people in a class
b. The text of a book
c. The storage of a continuously growing set of data
d. The grouping of many different, related items
e. The ordered storage of values so they can later be searched for quickly

3–10. Which expression will return a real number, given the following TYPE and VAR definitions, assuming the appropriate variables are previously defined?

```
TYPE
    Element = 1 .. 105;
    Name = ARRAY [1 .. 2] OF CHAR;

VAR
    Names : ARRAY [Element] OF Name;
    AtomicWeight : Array [Element] OF REAL;
```

a. AtomicWeight[Names[3]]
b. AtomicWeight[Element]
c. AtomicWeight(Element)
d. AtomicWeight(43)
e. AtomicWeight[3]

STRINGS

One type of packed array that is used quite often in Pascal is one involving CHAR. A packed array of CHAR is a string. In some other computer languages, a string is part of the language (for example, variables followed by a $ in BASIC). This is not so in Pascal. A string must be declared as follows:

```
TYPE
  Name = PACKED ARRAY [1 .. MAXINT] OF CHAR;
```

This defines a string variable called Name that would contain up to 32767 characters.

String Operations

Once declared, a string can undergo a number of operations. These operations would include, but not be limited to, the following:

1. Concatenation
2. String extraction
3. Matching

Concatenation is "string addition." This is not addition in a mathematical sense; it is rather the combination of two or more strings into a single string. The following is an example of a concatenation:

```
'John ' + 'E. ' + 'Parnell' = 'John E. Parnell'
```

String extraction involves just that—removal of a portion of a string. In the previous example, the middle initial could be extracted to yield *John Parnell*.

Matching involves searching a string for the presence or absence of a particular set of characters. Matching and string extraction could be combined to perform such functions as removing students names from a class list when they drop the class or removing a person's salary from a list of employees.

EXERCISES

The following definitions apply to exercises 3–11 and 3–12.
The TYPE definition

PACKED ARRAY [1 .. 25] OF CHAR

is equivalent to

STRING[25]

3–11. Which of the following is equivalent to the TYPE definition:

>   Name = PACKED ARRAY [1 .. 10] OF CHAR;
>   Class = 1 .. 35;
>   Classes = (Math, Science, History, English);
>   StudentNames = ARRAY [Math .. English] OF ARRAY [1 .. 35]
>
>   OF Name;

   a. StudentNames = ARRAY [1 .. 4, 1 .. 10, 1 .. 35] OF CHAR;
   b. StudentNames = ARRAY [1 .. 10, 1 .. 4, 1 .. 35] OF CHAR;
   c. StudentNames = ARRAY [1 .. 4, 1 .. 35, 1 .. 10] OF CHAR;
   d. StudentNames = ARRAY [1 .. 10, 1 .. 35, 1 .. 4] OF CHAR;
   e. StudentNames = ARRAY [1 .. 35, 1 .. 4, 1 .. 10] OF CHAR;

3–12. Which of the following is *not* a valid Pascal statement, given the following variable definitions and assuming that the variables have been assigned a valid value?

>   Name : ARRAY [1 .. 10] OF CHAR;
>   Alpha : PACKED ARRAY [1 .. 10] OF CHAR;

   a. Alpha[10] := Name[1];
   b. WRITE (Alpha);
   c. Name[3] := Alpha[3];
   d. READLN (Alpha);
   e. READLN (Name);

The following program applies to exercises 3–13 through 3–16.

```
PROGRAM Sample;
TYPE
  Name = (First, Middle, Last);
  Alpha = PACKED ARRAY [1 .. 10] OF CHAR;

VAR
  FullName : ARRAY [First .. Last] OF Alpha;
```

BEGIN

...

END.

3–13. Which statement below will *not* produce an error in this program?

    a. READ (Alpha[3]);
    b. READLN (Name);
    c. READLN (FullName);
    d. READLN (FullName[First,4]);
    e. READLN (FullName(Middle));

3–14. Which statement will *not* produce an error in this program?

    a. FullName[First] := FullName[Middle, 6 .. 10] + FullName[Last, 1 .. 5];
    b. FullName[First] := FullName[Middle,3];
    c. FullName[First, 1 .. 2] := FullName[Last, 1] + FullName[Middle, 1];
    d. FullName[First, 1] := FullName[Last, 1] + FullName[Middle, 1];
    e. FullName[First] := FullName[Middle];

3–15. How many characters maximum may be stored in FullName?

    a. 3
    b. 10
    c. 30
    d. 100
    e. It is unlimited.

3–16. What is the best equivalent statement to the VAR declaration of FullName?

    a. FullName : ARRAY [l .. 3] OF String$[1 .. 10];
    b. FullName : ARRAY [1 .. 3] OF String[1 .. 10];
    c. FullName : ARRAY [1 .. 3] OF String$[10];
    d. FullName : ARRAY [1 .. 3] OF String[10];
    e. None of the above.

3–17. If an employer has 10 employees and he wants his computer to keep their names alphabetically by the last, first, and middle name, which of the following formats is best suited for storing the names?

    a. Ten packed arrays of characters (strings).
    b. Thirty packed arrays of characters (strings).

c. A one-dimensional array of characters.

d. A one-dimensional array of packed arrays of characters (strings).

e. A two-dimensional array of strings.

3–18. Which of the following uses is best suited to strings?

a. The text of a book.

b. A computerized address book.

c. Number crunching.

d. Fast alphabetical storage and retrieval for a large data base.

e. The list of names of students in a class.

3–19. Which line of the following listing of a program will cause an error?

```
    PROGRAM Sample (INPUT, OUTPUT);

        TYPE
a.  Alpha = PACKED ARRAY [1 .. 25] OF CHAR;

        VAR
b.  FullName, First, Last : Alpha;

        BEGIN
            READLN (First);
            READLN (Last);
            FullName := Last;
c.      FullName[13] := ',';
d.      FullName[14 .. 25] := First[1 .. 12];
e.      WRITELN (FullName)
        END.
```

3–20. If the TYPE string were defined as follows, which answer would be a PROCEDURE that would return in one of the passed variable parameters the concatenation of the other two passed parameters?

```
        String = RECORD
            Data : PACKED ARRAY [1 .. 100] OF CHAR;
            Length : 0 .. 100
        END;

a.  PROCEDURE Concatenation (First, Second : String; VAR Final
    : String);

        VAR
            Count : 0 .. 100;

        BEGIN (* Concatenation *)
```

```
      IF (First.Length   0)
        THEN
          FOR Count := 1 TO First.Length DO
            Final.Data[Count] := First.Data[Count];
        IF (Second.Length   0)
          THEN
            FOR Count := First.Length + 1 TO First.Length
            + Second.Length DO
              Final.Data[Count] := Second.Data[Count −
              First.Length];
        Final.Length := First.Length + Second.Length
      END; (* Concatenation *)
```

b. PROCEDURE Concatenation (First, Second : String; VAR Final
: String);

```
  VAR
    Count : 0 .. 100;

  BEGIN (* Concatenation *)
    IF (First.Length   0)
      THEN
        FOR Count := 1 TO First.Length DO
          Final.Data[Count] := First.Data[Count];
    IF (Second.Length 0)
      THEN
        FOR Count := First.Length + 1 TO First.Length
        + Second.Length DO
          Final.Data[Count] := Second.Data[Count
          − First.Length]
  END; (* Concatenation *)
```

c. PROCEDURE Concatenation (First, Second : String; VAR Final
: String);

```
    VAR
      Count : 0 .. 100;

    BEGIN (* Concatenation *)
      IF (First.Length   0)
        THEN
          FOR Count := 1 TO First.Length DO
            Final.Data[Count] := First.Data[Count];
      IF (Second.Length   0)
        THEN
          FOR Count := 1 TO Second.Length DO
```

```
        Final.Data[Count] := Second.Data[Count];
      Final.Length := First.Length + Second.Length
    END; (* Concatenation *)
```

d. PROCEDURE Concatenation (First, Second : String; VAR Final
   : String);

```
    VAR
      Count : 0 .. 100;
    BEGIN (* Concatenation *)
      IF (First.Length   0)
        THEN
          FOR Count := 1 TO First.Length DO
            Final.Data[Count] := First.Data[Count];
      IF (Second.Length   0)
        THEN
          FOR Count := 1 TO Second.Length DO
            Final.Data[Count] := Second.Data[Count
              − First.Length]
    END; (* Concatenation *)
```

e. PROCEDURE Concatenation (First, Second : String; VAR Final
   : String);

```
    VAR
      Count : 0 .. 100;
    BEGIN (* Concatenation *)
      IF (First.Length ⟩ 0)
        THEN
          FOR Count := 1 TO First. Length DO
            Final.Data[Count] := First.Data[Count]
        ELSE
          IF (Second.Length ⟩ 0)
            THEN
              FOR Count := 1 TO Second.Length DO
                Final.Data[Count] := Second.Data[Count
                  − First.Length]
    END; (* Concatenation *)
```

LINKED LISTS

Adding or deleting characters to strings is somewhat cumbersome. Adding
characters to the array, assuming that there is sufficient room to add the
extra characters, involves shifting the position of all characters located

after the intended position by the number of characters in the additional segment. For example, to add the characters *E-period-space* to the name *John Parnell* involves shifting the word *Parnell* downward in the array by three positions. Deleting characters from a string involves shifting the characters after the point of deletion forward the required number of positions.

A more efficient way of altering the contents of an array is with linked lists. Linked lists involve the use of pointers. Each element in the list has two parts, or nodes. One node contains the piece of data itself, while the second node points to the location of the next data item. Diagrammatically, a linked list could be represented as follows:

value   value   value   value

pointer   pointer   pointer   pointer

There is a problem. How does the computer know where the beginning of the list is? The "Head" pointer points to the first item. The last pointer contains a "Null."

To use linked lists, you must so declare their existence. To do so, you declare the pointer. In the following example, "Person" is declared to be a pointer to information in PersonData.

```
TYPE
    Person = PersonData;
```

PersonData also must be defined.

```
TYPE
    PersonData = RECORD
        Name : String;
        Street : String;
        City : String;
        State : SmString;
        ZipCode : INTEGER:
        Pointer : Person
    END;
```

In the previous declaration, String and SmString need to be declared, too. We must also declare the first pointer.

```
TYPE
    String = PACKED ARRAY [1 .. 30] OF CHAR;
    SmString = PACKED ARRAY [1 .. 2] OF CHAR;

VAR
    Head : Person;
```

Within the program, Head is given its initial value.

```
BEGIN
    ...
    Head := NIL;
    ...
```

Then, as the program progresses, the value of Head is changed. So long as it is assigned a value of NIL, the list is empty.

In the list, nodes are allocated by using the predefined procedure NEW. The format of this procedure is as follows:

```
NEW(Head);
```

This procedure call creates a new node that is referenced by Head. To assign a value from the keyboard to the first field of the node, write:

```
READLN(Student);
Node ↑ .Name := Student;
```

Following the identifier Node is a caret, a period, and another identifier. This tells the computer to take the value stored in Student and assign it to the field Name pointed to by Node. Since Head was just used by NEW to create a node, it points to the first node. These statements are followed by statements assigning values to the other fields of PersonData.

The following is a complete program using linked lists.

```
PROGRAM Demo (INPUT);

    CONST
        MaxLength = 30;
    TYPE
        SmString = PACKED ARRAY [1 .. 2] OF CHAR;
```

```
String = PACKED ARRAY [1 .. MaxLength] OF CHAR;
PersonData = RECORD
    Name : String;
    Street : String;
    City : String;
    State : SmString;
    ZipCode : INTEGER;
    Pointer : Person
  END;


VAR
  Head : Person;
  Node : Person;
  Student : String;
  WhichStreet : String;
  WhichCity : String;
  WhichState : SmString;
  WhatZipCode : INTEGER;
  Counter : INTEGER;


BEGIN
  Head := NIL;

FOR Counter := 1 TO 10 DO
  BEGIN
    READLN(Student);
    READLN(WhichStreet);
    READLN(WhichCity);
    READLN(WhichState);
    READLN(WhatZipCode);
    NEW(Node);
    Node ↑ .Name := Student;
    Node ↑ .Street := WhichStreet;
    Node ↑ .City := WhichCity;
    Node ↑ .State := WhichState;
    Node ↑ .ZipCode := WhichZipCode;
    Node ↑ .Pointer := Head;
    Person := Person.Pointer
  END
END.
```

EXERCISES

3–21. Which of the following best describes an application for which linked lists are well-suited?

    a. A long list of names, which is to be kept in alphabetical order and in which names will be added, changed or deleted
    b. The text of a book
    c. The recording of 100 items of data
    d. Three-dimensional graphics processing
    e. The ordered storage of a large set of data, in which the speed of recalling any piece of data must be very fast

3–22. Which of the following Pascal TYPE definitions is used to set up a linked list of real numbers?

```
a. Item = RECORD
        Pred : Item;
        Next : Item;
        Data : REAL
     END;
b. Element = Item;
   Item = RECORD
        Data : REAL
     END;
c. Element = Item;
   Item = RECORD
        Pred : Item;
        Next : Item;
        Data : REAL;
     END;
d. Element = RECORD;
   Item = RECORD
        Next : Item;
        Data : REAL;
     END;
e. Element = Item;
   Item = RECORD
        Next : Element;
        Data : REAL
     END;
```

For exercises 3–23 through 3–26, the following definitions are valid:

```
TYPE
  Item = RECORD
```

```
    Pred, Next : Item;
      Data : REAL
    END;

  VAR
    Count : INTEGER;
    List, P, Q : Item;
```

3–23. To what are these definitions best suited?

a. A linked list of real numbers
b. A binary tree of real numbers
c. A binary tree of pointers to real numbers
d. A linked list of linked lists of pointers to real numbers
e. A linked list of pointers to real numbers

3–24. Which of the following statements would be best to use as initialization of this linked list?

a. List ↑ := NIL;
b. List := NIL;
   List.Pred := NIL;
c. New(List);
d. New(List);
   List ↑ .Pred := NIL;
e. New(List ↑);

3–25. Which of the following functions checks to see whether the passed real number is in the list that is pointed to by "List"?

a. FUNCTION Contained (Passed : REAL) : BOOLEAN;

```
    VAR
      A : Item;

    BEGIN (* Contained *)
      A := List;;
      Contained := FALSE;
      WHILE ((Contained = FALSE) and (A ⟨⟩ NIL)) DO
        IF (A ↑ .Data = Passed)
        THEN Contained := TRUE
        ELSE A := A ↑ .Next
    END; (* Contained *)
```

b. FUNCTION Contained (Passed : REAL) : BOOLEAN;

```
VAR
  A : ↑ Item;

BEGIN (* Contained *)
  A := List;
  Contained := FALSE;
  WHILE ((Passed = FALSE) AND (A ⟨⟩ NIL)) DO
    IF (A↑.Data = Passed)
      THEN Contained := TRUE
      ELSE A := A↑.Next
END; (* Contained *)
```

c. FUNCTION Contained (Passed : REAL) : BOOLEAN;

```
VAR
  A : ITEM;

BEGIN (* Contained *)
  A := List;
  Contained := FALSE;
  WHILE ((Contained = FALSE) AND (A ⟩⟨ NIL)) DO
    IF (A↑.Data = Passed)
      THEN Contained := TRUE
      ELSE A := A↑.Next
END; (* Contained *)
```

d. FUNCTION Contained (Passed : REAL) : BOOLEAN;

```
VAR
  A : Item;

BEGIN (* Contained *)
  A := List;
  Contained := FALSE;
  WHILE ((Passed = FALSE) AND (A ⟩⟨ NIL)) DO
    IF (A↑.Data = Passed)
      THEN Contained := TRUE
END; (* Contained *)
```

e. FUNCTION Contained (Passed : REAL) : BOOLEAN;

```
VAR
  A : Item;
```

```
BEGIN (* Contained *)
  A := List;
  Contained := FALSE;
  WHILE ((Contained = FALSE) AND (A >< NIL)) DO
    IF (A ↑ .Data = Passed)
      THEN Contained := TRUE
END; (* Contained *)
```

3–26. Which of the following statements would be valid in a standard Pascal program with the aforementioned definitions, assuming that the appropriate variables have been defined?

    a. Count := List ↑ .Data ;
    b. List ↑ .Pred := P ↑ .Next;
    c. P ↑ .Data := Count;
    d. P ↑ .Data := Q ↑ .Data ↑ ;
    e. List := P ↑ .Next ↑ ;

3–27. What is the difference between a linked list and a binary tree?

    a. A linked list has one or two nodes, but a binary tree has more than two nodes per item in the tree.
    b. A binary tree contains two linked lists.
    c. A linked list contains many binary trees.
    d. A linked list has a linear format (one thing comes after another), whereas a binary tree has two subitems under each item.
    e. A linked list has the ability to store only half of what can be stored in a binary tree.

3–28. Which of the following diagrams shows a single linked list?

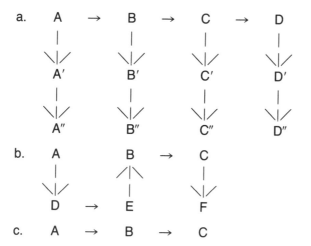

d.   A   →   B   →   C   →   D

e.   A   ←   B   →   C

3–29. Which of the following data types is illegal in standard Pascal?

a. A = PACKED RECORD
       B, C : A;
       D, E, F, G : INTEGER;
       H, I, J : REAL
    END;
b. A = PACKED RECORD
       B : A;
       D, E, F, G : INTEGER;
       H, I : REAL
    END;
c. A = RECORD
       B : A
    END;
d. A = RECORD
       B, C : A
    END;
e. A = PACKED RECORD
       B, C : INTEGER;
       D, E : INTEGER;
       F, G : REAL;
       H, I : REAL;
       J : A
    END;

3–30. Which of the following could not be used as the type definition of the nodes of a linked list?

a. A = PACKED RECORD
       B, C : A;
       D, E, F, G : INTEGER;
       H, I, J : REAL
    END;
b. A = PACKED RECORD
       D, E, F, G : INTEGER;
       H, I : REAL
    END;
c. A = RECORD
       B : A
    END;

d. A = RECORD
    B, C : A
  END;

e. A = PACKED RECORD
    B, C : INTEGER;
    D, E : INTEGER;
    F, G : REAL;
    H, I : REAL;
    J : A
  END;

STACKS

A fourth type of linear data structure is a stack. A stack is a dynamic data structure. It may increase or decrease in size as the program progresses. When items are placed onto the stack, they are PUSHed. When removed, they are POPped. However, additions and deletions may be made only from one end. Changes in the stack follow the *filo* rule, that is, first in, last out.

A stack is similar to a linked list in that as items are added to the beginning of the list, the initial pointer (usually referred to as TOP) is readjusted to point to the new item. A pointer in the new item points to the former first item. When items are removed from the list, TOP is adjusted so that it will point to the current top item.

In Pascal, a stack may be defined as a RECORD.

```
TYPE
  Stack = RECORD
      ZipCode : ARRAY [1 .. MAXINT] OF INTEGER;
      Top : 0 .. MAXINT
    END;

VAR
  Sstack : Stack;
```

In this example, the stack is called Sstack. It consists of up to 32767 zip codes, which are integers. Top represents the topmost zip code. In an empty stack, Top is equal to zero. When there is one zip code on the stack, Top is equal to one. When there are 10 zip codes, Top is equal to 10, and so on. Initially, there are no zip codes in the stack, so Sstack. Top := 0.

Within a program, to remove (POP) a value from a stack, you merely reassign the location of the Top pointer.

```
Sstack.Top := Sstack.Top  - 1
```

However, if the stack is empty when a POP operation is attempted, a run-time error is generated. As with other run—time errors, at this point, either the program aborts or it continues, perhaps with unexpected results. Which path is followed depends on the specific compiler being used, but neither one is desirable. Therefore, prior to a POP, it is wise to check the condition of the stack. This can be done with the following statement:

```
IF Sstack.Top = 0
THEN FirstCondition := TRUE
ELSE FirstCondition := FALSE;
```

This statement may either be included just before the POP as written, or it may be rewritten as a FUNCTION. The following is one example of how this function might look:

```
FUNCTION FirstCondition (Sstack : Stack) : Boolean;

  BEGIN
    IF Sstack.Top =0
      THEN FirstCondition := TRUE
      ELSE FirstCondition := FALSE
  END;
```

In this function, the value of Sstack is to be passed to the function, but not changed in value. Hence its declaration is not preceded by VAR. FirstCondition takes on a logical value of either TRUE or FALSE; hence, it is declared as Boolean.

Pop can also be written as a function.

```
FUNCTION Pop (VAR Sstack : Stack) : INTEGER;

  BEGIN
    FirstCondition(Sstack);
    IF FirstCondition
    THEN WRITELN ('Stack is empty.')
    ELSE
      BEGIN
        Pop := Sstack.ZipCode[Sstack.Top];
        Sstack.Top := Sstack.Top  - 1
      END
  END;
```

In this function, the value of Sstack, in particular the value of Sstack.Top, is to be changed by the function. Therefore, its declaration is preceded by VAR. The value of Pop is to be an integer, a zip code.

A PUSH can be written as a PROCEDURE.

```
PROCEDURE Push (VAR Sstack : Stack; Zip : INTEGER);

  BEGIN
    Sstack := Sstack + 1;
    Sstack.ZipCode := Zip
  END;
```

Again, an unexpected error can be generated. What if there are already 32767 zip codes in the list? You can't put on another one. You must test for this condition.

```
FUNCTION SecondCondition (Sstack : Stack) : Boolean;

  BEGIN
    IF Sstack.Top = MAXINT
      THEN SecondCondition := TRUE
      ELSE SecondCondition := FALSE
  END;
```

Again, we are passing the values of Sstack to the function without wanting to change any of its components. The value of SecondCondition is to be either TRUE or FALSE, hence the Boolean declaration.

Procedure Push should, therefore, be rewritten.

```
PROCEDURE Push (VAR Sstack : Stack; Zip : INTEGER);

  BEGIN
    SecondCondition(Sstack);
    IF SecondCondition
      THEN WRITELN ('Stack is too large.')
      ELSE
        BEGIN
          Sstack := Sstack + 1;
          Sstack.ZipCode := Zip
        END
  END;
```

The value of Zip is determined in the main body of the program.

The previous procedure could be altered slightly to have the value of Zip pushed onto the stack any number of times. In the following example, the value is placed onto the stack twice:

```
PROCEDURE Pusher (VAR Sstack : Stack; Zip : INTEGER);

    VAR
      Counter : INTEGER;

    BEGIN
      Counter := 1;
      WHILE (Counter ⟨ 3) AND NOT SecondCondition(Sstack)DO
        BEGIN
          Counter := Counter + 1;
          Sstack := Sstack + 1;
          Sstack.ZipCode := Zip
        END
    END;
```

In this procedure, note the function call. The call and test was done in a single statement. The following two are equivalent:

```
SecondCondition(Sstack);
WHILE (Counter ⟨ 3) AND NOT SecondCondition

WHILE (Counter ⟨ 3) AND NOT SecondCondition(Sstack)
```

EXERCISES

For exercises 3–31 through 3–33, assume that:

1. The PROCEDURE Push causes its arguments to be pushed onto the stack.
2. The FUNCTION Popper returns the sum of the two numbers popped from the stack.
3. The PROCEDURE Add causes its argument to be added to the number popped from the stack, and this sum is pushed twice.
4. The FUNCTION Subtract returns its argument subtracted from the number popped from the stack.
5. Answer is an INTEGER variable.

3–31. What is the value of Answer after these statements are executed?

    Push(10);
    Push(2);
    Add(2);
    Answer := Subtract(Popper);

    a. 12
    b. 8
    c. 6
    d. 4
    e. 2

3–32. How many numbers are on the stack after these operations?

    Push(10);
    Push(10);
    Answer := Popper;
    Push(2);
    Answer := Subtract(1);
    Push(123);
    Add(3);
    Add(1);

    a. 0
    b. 1
    c. 2
    d. 3
    e. 4

3–33. What number is still on the stack after these operations?

    Push(1);
    Push(2);
    Push(3);
    Push(4);
    Push(5);
    Push(6);
    Push(7);
    Add(Popper + Subtract(1) + Popper);
    Answer := Popper;

a. No numbers are left on the stack.

b. 1

c. 24

d. 25

e. 48

3–34. A stack follows which of the following rules?

a. First in, first out

b. First in, last out

c. Last in, last out

d. Every pop precedes its push.

e. Every push has at least one pop.

For questions 3–35 through 3–38, assume that:

1. The PROCEDURE Push pushes its argument onto the stack TWICE.
2. The PROCEDUREs Add and Multiply pop the last two numbers on the stack, perform the applicable operation on those numbers, and push the answer back onto the stack.
3. The FUNCTION Pop returns a number popped from the stack.
4. Answer is an INTEGER variable.

3–35. How many numbers are on the stack when it is the biggest during these operations?

Push(124);
Push(342);
Add;
Push(12);
Push(2);
Add;
Push(2);
Mutliply;
Add;
Add;

a. 4

b. 6

c. 7

d. 8

e. 10

3–36. What is the last number that can be popped after these operations?

Push(12);
Add;
Push(12);
Answer := Pop;
Add;

a. 12

b. 24

c. 36

d. 48

e. There are no numbers left on the stack.

3–37. How many actual pushes are performed during these operations?

Push(1);
Push(2);
Add;
Add;

a. 2

b. 4

c. 6

d. 8

e. Cannot be determined from the information given.

3–38. What is the sum of the numbers on the stack after these operations?

Push(1);
Push(1);
Push(1);
Push(1);
Push(1);
Add;
Add;
Add;

Add;

Add;

Multiply;

a. 4

b. 5

c. 9

d. 10

e. 25

The following applies to questions 3–39 and 3–40: A stack in a computer can be compared to a pile of papers. The answers for 3–39 and 3–40 are to be taken from these answers.

a. Putting a sheet of paper on the bottom of the pile

b. Putting a sheet of paper on the top of the pile

c. Replacing the sheet of paper on the bottom with a new one

d. Taking the sheet of paper on the top

e. Putting a new sheet just under the last sheet pushed

3–39. What is the equivalent of a PUSH operation?

3–40. What is the equivalent of a POP operation?

QUEUES

Another type of linear data structure is a queue. Like a stack, a queue is a dynamic data structure. It also increases and decreases in size. However, queues follow a *fifo* pattern of insertion and deletion. This is first in, first out. Items are added to one end of the list and removed only from the other end. This is much like the first come, first served rule that is followed by many business establishments.

PROCEDURE Push could be used when dealing with queues. However, FUNCTION Pop could not. In Pop, items are taken off the series in reverse order of their addition. Pop could be modified to work with queues.

```
FUNCTION PopQueue (VAR Sstack : Stack) : INTEGER;

    VAR
        Counter : INTEGER;
```

```
BEGIN
  If FirstCondition(Sstack)
    THEN WRITELN ('Queue is empty.')
    ELSE
      BEGIN
        PopQueue := Sstack.ZipCode[1];
        Counter := 0;
        WHILE (Sstack.Top ⟨ 32767) DO
          BEGIN
            Counter := Counter + 1;
            Sstack.ZipCode[Counter] := Sstack.ZipCode[Counter + 1]
          END
      END
END;
```

In the previous PROCEDURE, the purpose of the WHILE loop is to shift the values forward one position. This could be somewhat time-consuming when you are dealing with a long queue.

EXERCISES

3–41. Which of the following best describes the actions of a queue?

  a. The first item placed onto a queue is stored "in the queue." The next item placed onto the queue pushes the last one back, and thus becomes the first item on the queue.

  b. The first item placed onto a queue is the first one to be retrieved.

  c. The first item placed onto a queue is the first one to be retrieved. However, if, for example, five items are placed on the queue, and the first two are retrieved, then another item is added, this new item will be retrieved before the other three items will be.

  d. Queue is a synonym for stack.

  e. The queue is Pascal's substitute for BASIC's string variables.

3–42. Which of the following is a best application for a queue?

  a. Using a queue instead of a stack in computer programming

  b. Using a queue to keep track of the current balance in a savings and checking account

c. Using a queue to keep a list of things that must be done by the computer

d. Using a queue for inventory control in a small to midsized business

e. Using a queue for a large data base of words, as for a dictionary

The following definitions apply to questions 3–43 through 3–45.

```
TYPE
  QueueType = Element;
  Element = RECORD
       Next : QueueType;
       Data : INTEGER
     END:

VAR
  Queue : QueueType;
```

3–43. Which of the following routines takes an integer off the queue defined below, if all the variables involved have already been defined?

a. FUNCTION GetFromQueue (QueueName : QueueType) : INTE-GER;

```
     VAR
       Count : INTEGER;

     BEGIN (* GetFromQueue *)
       Count := 1;
       WHILE (Count 〈 QueueName.Data) DO
         Count := Count + 1;
       GetFromQueue := Count
     END; (* GetFromQueue *)
```

b. FUNCTION GetFromQueue (QueueName : QueueType) : INTE-GER;

```
     VAR
       Count : INTEGER;
```

```
    BEGIN (* GetFromQueue *)
      Count := 1;
      WHILE (Count 〈 QueueName.Data) DO
        Count := Count + 1;
      GetFromQueue := Count;
      QueueName := QueueName.Next
    END; (* GetFromQueue *)
```

c. FUNCTION GetFromQueue (QueueName : QueueType) : INTE-
   GER;

```
    BEGIN (* GetFromQueue *)
      GetFromQueue := QueueName.Data;
      QueueName := QueueName.Next
    END; (* GetFromQueue *)
```

d. FUNCTION GetFromQueue (QueueName : QueueType) : INTE-
   GER;

```
    BEGIN (* GetFromQueue *)
      QueueName := QueueName.Next;
      GetFromQueue := QueueName.Data
    END; (* GetFrom Queue *)
```

e. FUNCTION GetFromQueue (VAR QueueName : QueueType) :
   INTEGER;

```
    BEGIN (* GetFromQueue *)
      GetFromQueue := QueueName.Data;
      QueueName := QueueName.Next
    END; (* GetFromQueue *)
```

3–44. Which of the following routines is used to add an integer to this
queue?

a. PROCEDURE AddToQueue (VAR QueueName : QueueType;
   Addition : INTEGER);

```
    VAR
      OldQueue : QueueType;
```

```
    BEGIN (* AddToQueue *)
      OldQueue := QueueName;
      New(QueueName);
      QueueName.Next := OldQueue;
      QueueName.Data := Addition
    END; (* AddToQueue *)
```

b. PROCEDURE AddToQueue (QueueName : QueueType; Addition : INTEGER);

```
    VAR
      OldQueue : QueueType;

    BEGIN (* AddToQueue *)
      OldQueue := QueueName;
      New(QueueName);
      QueueName.Next := OldQueue;
      QueueName.Data := Addition
    END; (* AddToQueue *)
```

c. PROCEDURE AddToQueue (QueueName : QueueType; Addition : INTEGER);

```
    VAR
      OldQueue : QueueType;

    BEGIN (* AddToQueue *)
      OldQueue := QueueName;
      New(QueueName);
      OldQueue.Next := OldQueue;
      OldQueue.Data := Addition
    END; (* AddToQueue *)
```

d. PROCEDURE AddToQueue (VAR QueueName : QueueType; Addition : INTEGER);

```
    VAR
      OldQueue : QueueType;

    BEGIN (* AddToQueue *)
      QueueName := OldQueue;
```

```
      New(oldQueue);
      OldQueue.Next := OldQueue;
      OldQueue.Data := Addition
   END; (* AddToQueue *)
```

e. PROCEDURE AddToQueue (QueueName : QueueType; Addition : INTEGER);

```
   VAR
      OldQueue : QueueType;

   BEGIN (* AddToQueue *)
      OldQueue := QueueName;
      WHILE (OldQueue.Next ()NIL) DO
         Oldqueue := OldQueue.Next;
      New(OldQueue.Next);
      OldQueue.Next.Data := Addition
   END; (* AddToQueue *)
```

3–45. Which of the following routines returns the sum of the entire queue and adds this sum to the queue itself, assuming the proper procedure from the previous problem has already been defined?

a. PROCEDURE Sum (QueueName : QueueType);

```
   VAR
      QueuePointer : QueueType;
      Summation : INTEGER;

   BEGIN (* Sum *)
      QueuePointer := QueueName;
      Summation := 0;
      WHILE (QueuePointer () NIL) DO
         BEGIN (* WHILE loop *)
            Summation := Summation + QueuePointer.Data;
            QueuePointer := QueuePointer.Next
         END; (*WHILE loop *)
      AddToQueue (QueueName, Summation)
   END; (* Sum *)
```

b. PROCEDURE Sum (VAR QueueName : QueueType);

```
VAR
  QueuePointer : QueueType;
  Summation : INTEGER:

BEGIN (* Sum *)
  QueuePointer := QueueName;
  Summation := 0;
  WHILE (QueueName 〈〉 NIL) DO
    BEGIN (* WHILE loop *)
      Summation := Summation + QueueName.Data;
      QueueName := QueueName.Next
    END; (* WHILE loop *)
  AddToQueue (QueueName, Summation)
END; (* Sum *)
```

c. PROCEDURE Sum (VAR QueueName : QueueType);

```
VAR
  QueuePointer : QueueType;
  Summation : INTEGER:

BEGIN (* Sum *)
  QueuePointer := QueueName;
  Summation := 0;
  WHILE (QueueName 〈〉 NIL) DO
    BEGIN (* WHILE loop *)
      Summation := Summation + QueueName.Data;
      QueuePointer := QueuePointer.Next
    END:
  AddToQueue (QueueName, Summation)
END; (* Sum *)
```

d. PROCEDURE Sum (QueueName : QueueType);

```
VAR
  QueuePointer : QueueType;
  Summation : INTEGER;

BEGIN (* Sum *)
  QueuePointer := QueueName;
  Summation := 0;
```

```
    WHILE (QueuePointer ()NIL) DO
      BEGIN (* WHILE loop *)
        Summation := Summation + QueuePointer.Data;
        QueuePointer := QueuePointer.Next
      END; (* WHILE loop *)
    AddToQueue (QueuePointer, Summation)
  END; (* Sum *)
```

e. PROCEDURE Sum (QueueName : QueueType);

```
  VAR
    QueuePointer : QueueType;
    Summation : INTEGER;

  BEGIN (*Sum *)
    QueuePointer := QueueName;
    Summation := 0;
    WHILE (QueuePointer () NIL) DO
      BEGIN (* WHILE loop *)
        Summation := Summation + QueueName.Data;
        QueuePointer := QueuePointer.Next
      END; (* WHILE loop *)
    AddToQueue (QueueName, Summation)
  END; (* Sum *)
```

For questions 3–46 through 3–48, the following definitions apply:

1. Put is a PROCEDURE that adds its argument to the queue.
2. Take is a FUNCTION that returns the current value "on the queue."
3. Add is a PROCEDURE that takes a number from the queue, adds it to its own argument, and puts the sum on the queue.
4. Subtract is a FUNCTION that takes a number from the queue, subtracts it from its own argument, and returns the difference.
5. Answer is an INTEGER variable.

3–46. What will be in Answer after these statements are executed?

```
    Put(2);
    Add(3);
    Answer := Subtract(6);
```

a. 1
b. 2
c. 3
d. 4
e. 5

3–47. What will be contained in Answer after the following statements
are executed?

Put(2);
Put(4);
Add(5);
Put(Subtract(10));
Answer := Take;

a. 1
b. 2
c. 6
d. 7
e. 8

3–48. What will be on the queue after these operations?

Put(1);
Put(2);
Put(3);
Add(4);
Answer := Subtract(5) + Take;

a. 1
b. 2
c. 3
d. 5
e. 6

The following applies to questions 3–49 and 3–50: A queue in a computer
can be compared to a pile of papers. The following are the possible answers
for questions 3–49 and 3–50.

a. Putting a sheet of paper on the bottom of the pile
b. Putting a sheet of paper on the top of the pile

c. Replacing the sheet of paper on the bottom with a new one

d. Taking the sheet of paper on the top

e. Taking the sheet of paper on the bottom

3–49. Which of the above is the equivalent of adding a number onto the queue?

3–50. Which of the above is the equivalent of retrieving a number from the queue?

TREES

A tree is a special type of linked list. It differs from a standard linked list in that the elements do not have a linear pointer system. In a standard linked list, the pointers point only to the next member of the list. (In the case of a doubly linked list, one pointer points to the following element and one points to the previous element.) In a tree, it is possible to work back to the base element, the root from any of a number of other elements, called nodes.

The following diagram helps illustrate the various parts of a tree:

In this diagram, A is the root of the tree. From A there are two branches, each leading to a subtree. B and C are children of A, siblings of each other, and parents of D, E, F and G, H, I, respectively. D, E, and F are siblings. Since they are without children, they are called terminal nodes, or leaves. G, H, and I are also siblings. H, itself, has two children, J and K. G, I, J, and K are also terminal nodes, or leaves.

When the nodes of the tree have only two offspring, the tree becomes a binary tree. The following is an illustration of a binary tree:

Even though there are only two branches coming off each node, a binary tree still has all the parts of a general tree. In the new diagram, A is the root; B and C are its children. D, E, F, H, and I are terminal nodes, or leaves. The tree headed by node B is a subtree, specifically the left subtree. The tree headed by node C is the right subtree. Each offspring can also be referred to by whether it is the left or right offspring. D is the left offspring and E is the right offspring of parent B.

  The order of the offspring is important. The following diagram represents two distinct binary trees:

EXERCISES

3–51. Given the following binary tree, indicate the following:

  a. the root

  b. the leaves

  c. sets of siblings

  d. children of the root

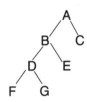

3–52. Indicate the number of binary trees possible, given the following number of nodes.

  a. 0

  b. 1

  c. 2

  d. 3

  e. 4

3–53. For the previous question, draw all the possible binary trees.

4

Basic Logic

Basic algorithms used in computer science fall into one of three types. These types are sequential, iterative, and recursive.

SEQUENTIAL ALGORITHMS

Sequential algorithms involve the execution of a set of statements from top to bottom, in a single pass. This type of algorithm does not involve loops, GOTOS, PROCEDURES, or FUNCTIONS.

ITERATIVE ALGORITHMS

Iterative algorithms involve various types of looping structures. These structures include FOR, WHILE, and REPEAT, or a combination thereof.

RECURSIVE ALGORITHMS

Recursion occurs when a particular subprogram calls itself, that is, within the subprogram is a procedure call for itself. An example of recursion is the determination of the exponentiation of a number. In Pascal, the standard function SQR returns the square of the argument. To obtain any other power requires a calculation. This could be done through recursion.

SORTING

Quite often in computer science, you must sort a list of data into some order. The following is a brief discussion of the more common sorting algorithms.

Bubble (Exchange) Sort

In a bubble (exchange) sort, each member of the list to be sorted is compared with every other member of the list, with an appropriate exchange of values occurring whenever the values are out of the desired order. If the list contains 10 values (A[1], A[2], A[3], ..., A[10]), then A[1] is compared to A[2], A[3], ..., A[10]. After this is done, A[2] is compared to A[3], A[4], ..., A[10]. The sort proceeds this way until every element in the list has been compared to every other element. Whenever comparisons reveal that the elements are out of the desired order, then their values are exchanged.

The following is an illustration of the bubble sort. In this illustration, those elements being compared are bracketed. If the elements are to be switched, there is an S after the bracket.

A[1]	6	2	2	2	2	2	2	1	1	1
A[2]	2	6	6	6	6	6	6	6	6	6
A[3]	4	4	4	4	4	4	4	4	4	4
A[4]	8	8	8	8	8	8	8	8	8	8
A[5]	9	9	9	9	9	9	9	9	9	9
A[6]	6	6	6	6	6	6	6	6	6	6
A[7]	5	5	5	5	5	5	5	5	5	5
A[8]	1	1	1	1	1	1	1	2	2	2
A[9]	3	3	3	3	3	3	3	3	3	3
A[10]	7	7	7	7	7	7	7	7	7	7

(First comparison A[1]/A[2]: S. Later comparison A[8]/A[9] region: S)

A[1]	1	1	1	1	1	1	1	1	1
A[2]	6	4	4	4	4	4	2	2	2
A[3]	4	6	6	6	6	6	6	6	6
A[4]	8	8	8	8	8	8	8	8	8
A[5]	9	9	9	9	9	9	9	9	9
A[6]	6	6	6	6	6	6	6	6	6
A[7]	5	5	5	5	5	5	5	5	5

(Comparison A[2]/A[3]: S; later A[5] region: S)

A[8]	2	2	2	2	2	2	4	4	4
A[9]	3	3	3	3	3	3	3	3	3
A[10]	7	7	7	7	7	7	7	7	7

A[1]	1	1	1	1		1		1		1	1
A[2]	2	2	2	2		2		2		2	2
A[3]	6	6	6	6		5		4		3	3
A[4]	8	8	8	8		8		8		8	8
A[5]	9	9	9	9	S	9	S	9		9	9
A[6]	6	6	6	6		6		6	S	6	6
A[7]	5	5	5	5		6		6		6	6
A[8]	4	4	4	4		4		5		5	5
A[9]	3	3	3	3		3		3		4	4
A[10]	7	7	7	7		7		7		7	7

A[1]	1	1		1	1		1		1	1
A[2]	2	2		2	2		2		2	2
A[3]	3	3		3	3		3		3	3
A[4]	8	8		6	6		5		4	4
A[5]	9	9	S	9	9		9		9	9
A[6]	6	6		8	8	S	8	S	8	8
A[7]	6	6		6	6		6		6	6
A[8]	5	5		5	5		6		6	6
A[9]	4	4		4	4		4		5	5
A[10]	7	7		7	7		7		7	7

A[1]	1		1		1	1		1	1
A[2]	2		2		2	2		2	2
A[3]	3		3		3	3		3	3
A[4]	4		4		4	4		4	4
A[5]	9	S	8		6	6		5	5
A[6]	8		9	S	9	9		9	9
A[7]	6		6		8	8	S	8	8
A[8]	6		6		6	6		6	6
A[9]	5		5		5	5		6	6
A[10]	7		7		7	7		7	7

A[1]	1	1	1	1	1
A[2]	2	2	2	2	2
A[3]	3	3	3	3	3
A[4]	4	4	4	4	4
A[5]	5	5	5	5	5
A[6]	9	8	6	6	6
A[7]	8	9	9	9	9
A[8]	6	6	8	8	8
A[9]	6	6	6	6	6
A[10]	7	7	7	7	7

A[1]	1	1	1	1
A[2]	2	2	2	2
A[3]	3	3	3	3
A[4]	4	4	4	4
A[5]	5	5	5	5
A[6]	6	6	6	6
A[7]	9	8	6	6
A[8]	8	9	9	9
A[9]	6	6	6	6
A[10]	7	7	7	7

A[1]	1	1	1
A[2]	2	2	2
A[3]	3	3	3
A[4]	4	4	4
A[5]	5	5	5
A[6]	6	6	6
A[7]	6	6	6
A[8]	9	8	7
A[9]	8	9	9
A[10]	7	7	8

A[1]	1	1
A[2]	2	2
A[3]	3	3

A[4]	4	4
A[5]	5	5
A[6]	6	6
A[7]	6	6
A[8]	7	7
A[9]	9 ⌉	8
A[10]	8 ⌋ S	9

In the bubble sort, given that there are N items to be sorted, there will be $(N - 1) + (N - 2) + (N - 3) + \ldots + (1)$ comparisons made, or approximately N^2. In the worst case (when a list is in direct reverse order of the desired condition), there will be $(N)(N - 1)/2$ or about $N^2/2$ switchings. In the average case, however, there will be only $(N)(N - 1)/4$, or $N^2/4$ switchings.

As you can see from the previous example, the bubble sort is so named because the smaller values move up (bubble up) the array. In reality, the same algorithm could be set up so that the larger items move up the array, but then we all know that heavier items tend to sink, not float. Don't they?

Insertion Sort

The insertion sort involves the use of a second array, equal in size to the array that is to be sorted. In this method, the first item of the unsorted array is assigned to the first element in the empty array. The value of the next item of the unsorted array is then compared to the first value in the new array. If the values are in correct order, then this new value is assigned to the next available space in the new array. If, however, they are out of order, then the value(s) in the new array are pushed down one position in the array, and the assignment is made to the empty spot in the array. This procedure is continued until all elements in the unsorted array have been placed into the new, now sorted, array.

Using the data from the bubble sort, the insertion sort progresses as follows. In this example, array A is the unsorted array, and B becomes the sorted array.

A[1]	6	→	B[1]	6
A[2]	2			
A[3]	4			
A[4]	8			
A[5]	9			

A[6]   6
A[7]   5
A[8]   1
A[9]   3
A[10]   7

A[1]   6   ⌐→   B[1]   2
A[2]   2   ⌡   B[2]   6
A[3]   4
A[4]   8
A[5]   9
A[6]   6
A[7]   5
A[8]   1
A[9]   3
A[10]   7

A[1]   6   B[1]   2
A[2]   2   ⌐→   B[2]   4
A[3]   4   ⌡   B[3]   6
A[4]   8
A[5]   9
A[6]   6
A[7]   5
A[8]   1
A[9]   3
A[10]   7

A[1]   6   B[1]   2
A[2]   2   B[2]   4
A[3]   4   B[3]   6
A[4]   8   →   B[4]   8
A[5]   9
A[6]   6
A[7]   5
A[8]   1

A[9]	3		
A[10]	7		

A[1]	6		B[1]	2
A[2]	2		B[2]	4
A[3]	4		B[3]	6
A[4]	8		B[4]	8
A[5]	9	→	B[5]	9
A[6]	6			
A[7]	5			
A[8]	1			
A[9]	3			
A[10]	7			

A[1]	6		B[1]	2
A[2]	2		B[2]	4
A[3]	4		B[3]	6
A[4]	8	⌐→	B[4]	6
A[5]	9		B[5]	8
A[6]	6	⌐	B[6]	9
A[7]	5			
A[8]	1			
A[9]	3			
A[10]	7			

A[1]	6		B[1]	2
A[2]	2		B[2]	4
A[3]	4	⌐→	B[3]	5
A[4]	8		B[4]	6
A[5]	9		B[5]	6
A[6]	6		B[6]	8
A[7]	5	⌐	B[7]	9
A[8]	1			
A[9]	3			
A[10]	7			

A[1]	6		B[1]	1
A[2]	2		B[2]	2
A[3]	4		B[3]	4
A[4]	8		B[4]	5
A[5]	9		B[5]	6
A[6]	6		B[6]	6
A[7]	5		B[7]	8
A[8]	1		B[8]	9
A[9]	3			
A[10]	7			

A[1]	6		B[1]	1
A[2]	2		B[2]	2
A[3]	4		B[3]	3
A[4]	8		B[4]	4
A[5]	9		B[5]	5
A[6]	6		B[6]	6
A[7]	5		B[7]	6
A[8]	1		B[8]	8
A[9]	3		B[9]	9
A[10]	7			

A[1]	6		B[1]	1
A[2]	2		B[2]	2
A[3]	4		B[3]	3
A[4]	8		B[4]	4
A[5]	9		B[5]	5
A[6]	6		B[6]	6
A[7]	5		B[7]	6
A[8]	1		B[8]	7
A[9]	3		B[9]	8
A[10]	7		B[10]	9

One disadvantage of this algorithm is that it requires space for a second array equal in size to the one being sorted. Another is that the location of the last filled element in the sorted array must be maintained and updated as each new element is added. This, too, requires space.

For a list consisting of N items to be sorted, the number of comparisons in the worst case is approximately $N^2/2$, whereas in the best case $(N - 1)$ comparisons are required. It should be noted that in the worst case, the list to be sorted is already sorted!

Pair Exchange Sort

The pair exchange sort is a version of the bubble sort. The main difference is that in the pair exchange sort, the comparisons are made only between one element and its immediate neighbor.

In this method, a counter is used to keep track of the number of passes made through the list. When this counter is odd, each item in an odd-numbered position (1, 3, 5) is compared with the element in the next even-numbered position (2, 4, 6). When this comparison is made, the larger value in the comparison is assigned to the even-numbered position.

During the even-numbered passes, the even-numbered positioned items (2, 4, 6) are compared with the next highest odd-numbered positioned item (3, 5, 7). When this comparison is made, the larger-valued item is assigned to the odd-numbered position.

Using the same array as in the bubble sort, the pair exchange sort looks like the following. Again, the brackets indicate the positional comparisons. The S indicates that a switch is to take place.

A[1]	6	2	2	2	2	2
A[2]	2	6	6	6	6	6
A[3]	4	4	4	4	4	4
A[4]	8	8	8	8	8	8
A[5]	9	9	9	6	6	6
A[6]	6	6	6	9	9	9
A[7]	5	5	5	5	1	1
A[8]	1	1	1	1	5	5
A[9]	3	3	3	3	3	3
A[10]	7	7	7	7	7	7
A[1]	2	2	2	2	2	
A[2]	6	4	4	4	4	
A[3]	4	6	6	6	6	

A[4]	8	8⎤	6	6	6
A[5]	6	6⎦	8	8	8
A[6]	9	9	9⎤	1	1
A[7]	1	1	1⎦	9	9
A[8]	5	5	5	5⎤	3
A[9]	3	3	3	3⎦	5
A[10]	7	7	7	7	7

A[1]	2⎤	2	2	2	2	2
A[2]	4⎦	4	4	4	4	4
A[3]	6	6⎤	6	6	6	6
A[4]	6	6⎦	6	6	6	6
A[5]	8	8	8⎤S	1	1	1
A[6]	1	1	1⎦	8	8	8
A[7]	9	9	9	9⎤S	3	3
A[8]	3	3	3	3⎦	9	9
A[9]	5	5	5	5	5⎤	5
A[10]	7	7	7	7	7⎦	7

A[1]	2	2	2	2	2
A[2]	4⎤	4	4	4	4
A[3]	6⎦	6	6	6	6
A[4]	6	6⎤S	1	1	1
A[5]	1	1⎦	6	6	6
A[6]	8	8	8⎤S	3	3
A[7]	3	3	3⎦	8	8
A[8]	9	9	9	9⎤S	5
A[9]	5	5	5	5⎦	9
A[10]	7	7	7	7	7

A[1]	2⎤	2	2	2	2	2
A[2]	4⎦	4	4	4	4	4
A[3]	6	6⎤S	1	1	1	1
A[4]	1	1⎦	6	6	6	6
A[5]	6	6	6⎤S	3	3	3
A[6]	3	3	3⎦	6	6	6

A[7]	8	8	8	8 ⎤ S	5	5
A[8]	5	5	5	5 ⎦	8	8
A[9]	9	9	9	9	9 ⎤ S	7
A[10]	7	7	7	7	7 ⎦	9

A[1]	2	2	2	2	2
A[2]	4 ⎤ S	1	1	1	1
A[3]	1 ⎦	4	4	4	4
A[4]	6	6 ⎤ S	3	3	3
A[5]	3	3 ⎦	6	6	6
A[6]	6	6	6 ⎤ S	5	5
A[7]	5	5	5 ⎦	6	6
A[8]	8	8	8	8 ⎤ S	7
A[9]	7	7	7	7 ⎦	8
A[10]	9	9	9	9	9

A[1]	2 ⎤ S	1	1	1	1	1
A[2]	1 ⎦	2	2	2	2	2
A[3]	4	4 ⎤ S	3	3	3	3
A[4]	3	3 ⎦	4	4	4	4
A[5]	6	6	6 ⎤ S	5	5	5
A[6]	5	5	5 ⎦	6	6	6
A[7]	6	6	6	6 ⎤	6	6
A[8]	7	7	7	7 ⎦	7	7
A[9]	8	8	8	8	8 ⎤	8
A[10]	9	9	9	9	9 ⎦	9

It took 7 passes, involving 32 comparisons, to sort this list. The bubble sort took 9 passes and 45 comparisons to sort the same list. However, in the best case—sorting a sorted list—the pair exchange requires at least two passes, one even and one odd, involving N comparisons. If no switchings occur, then the list is sorted. In the bubble sort, this would still require $(N - 1)$ passes and N^2 comparisons. In the worst case, $N^2/2$ comparisons are required in the pair exchange method of sorting, the same as for the bubble sort.

One drawback to this version of the exchange sort is that there is some additional overhead involved. A counter must be employed to keep track of the even-versus odd-numbered passes. This requires additional memory, as well as additional time to change its value periodically.

Quicksort

In the quicksort algorithm, one element is selected as a pivot. The values of all other elements are compared with that of the pivot. Those having a higher value are placed toward the end of the list. Those having a lower value are placed more toward the beginning of the list.

Ideally, the pivot chosen has as its value the median of the list. This is difficult to do in practice. Quite often, the pivot chosen is the element initially in the middle position of the unsorted list. The reason for this is that in choosing a position as pivot, there is a greater chance (however slight) that this will at least be close to the median value. (The first or last element proves to be a very poor pivot when the list is close to being sorted already.) If the values in the list are in a fairly random order, then no harm is done in choosing this middle value. Each element position in a random list has an equal chance of being the median value.

Once the pivot is chosen, the values in the list are shifted downward one position beginning with the first position and ending with the position immediately in front of the pivot position. This causes position 1 in the list to be free, that is, free to take on a new value.

The algorithm quicksort requires that two pointers be used. The first keeps track of the position of the element highest in the list that is to be compared with the pivot. The second is for the lowest. For the sake of this discussion, let the pointers be called First and Last, respectively. The algorithm has two parts.

First, the value of the element pointed to by Last is compared to Pivot. If Pivot is greater, then the value of the element is assigned to the free position. Last is then incremented by one. If Pivot were less, then Last is just incremented by one.

Second, the value of the element pointed to by First is compared to Pivot. If Pivot is greater, then First is incremented by one. If Pivot is less, then the element's value is assigned to the free position.

There is an alternation between parts 1 and 2 until First and Last meet, that is, until there is but one position between First and Last.

This set of procedures is then repeated again, but this time using only the part of the list greater than Pivot. (A new Pivot is chosen and new First and Last pointers are assigned.) Once this is completed, it is again repeated and repeated until the top of the list is in order. The procedures are then applied to the portions of the list below the Pivot value(s).

The following illustrates quicksort.

A[1]	6	—	—	3	3
A[2]	2	6 First	6 First	6 First	—
A[3]	4	2	2	2	2 First
A[4]	8	4	4	4	4
A[5]	9	8	8	8	8
A[6]	6 Pivot	9	9	9	9
A[7]	5	5	5	5	5
A[8]	1	1	1	1 Last	1 Last
A[9]	3	3	3 Last	—	6
A[10]	7	7 Last	7	7	7

A[1]	3	3	3	3	3
A[2]	1	1	1	1	1
A[3]	2 First	2	2	2	2
A[4]	4	4 First	4	4	4
A[5]	8	8	8 First	—	5
A[6]	9	9	9	9 First	9 First
A[7]	5 Last	5 Last	5 Last	5 Last	—
A[8]	—	—	—	8	8
A[9]	6	6	6	6	6
A[10]	7	7	7	7	7

A[1]	3	—	—	—	1
A[2]	1	3 First	3 First	3 First	3 First
A[3]	2 Pivot(N)	1	1	1 Last	—
A[4]	4	4	4 Last	4	4
A[5]	5	5 Last	5	5	5
A[6]	6 Pivot(O)	6	6	6	6
A[7]	9	9	9	9	9
A[8]	8	8	8	8	8
A[9]	6	6	6	6	6
A[10]	7	7	7	7	7

A[1]	1	1	1	1	1
A[2]	2	2	2	2	2
A[3]	3 Pivot(ON)	3	3	3	3
A[4]	4	4	4	4	4
A[5]	5	5	5	5	5
A[6]	6	—	—	7	7
A[7]	9	9	6 First	6 First	6
A[8]	8	8 Pivot(N)	9	9	9 First
A[9]	6	6	6	6 Last	6 Last
A[10]	7	7	7 Last	—	—

A[1]	1	1	1	1		1	
A[2]	2	2	2	2		2	
A[3]	3	3	3	3		3	
A[4]	4	4	4	4		4	
A[5]	5	5	5	5		5	
A[6]	7	7	7	7		—	
A[7]	6	6	6	6	Pivot(N)	7	First
A[8]	—	6	6	6		6	Last
A[9]	6 Last	—	8	8		8	
A[10]	9	9	9	9		9	

A[1]	1	1	1
A[2]	2	2	2
A[3]	3	3	3
A[4]	4	4	4
A[5]	5	5	5
A[6]	6	6	6
A[7]	7	—	6
A[8]	—	7	7
A[9]	8	8	8
A[10]	9	9	9

Radix Sort

The radix sorting algorithm involves the various digit positions within a number as the sorting key. In this algorithm, a sort is performed first using the ones column. The list is then resorted using the tens column. Then the hundreds, and so forth until the list is fully sorted.

Since there are 10 different possible values for each digit position (0 through 9), 10 separate matrices are required for this algorithm. (It is possible to use a single double-subscripted matrix in place of the 10 matrices.) The following illustrates the radix sorting algorithm.

The list to be sorted is:

21   53   23   08   23   85   38   69   70   04   88   50

On the first pass through the list, the numbers are placed into the matrices based on the lowest-order digit (that is, the ones column).

	0	1	2	3	4	5	6	7	8	9
				23					88	
	50			23					38	
	70	21		53	04	85			08	69
Matrix Position	0	1	2	3	4	5	6	7	8	9

These values are then reassigned to the original matrix, progressing from matrix zero to matrix nine, using *fifo*. The following is a partially sorted list:

70 50 21 53 23 23 04 85 08 38 88 69

On the second pass through the list, the numbers are placed back into the matrices based on the next lowest-order digit (the tens column).

	0	1	2	3	4	5	6	7	8	9
			23							
	08		23			53			88	
	04		21	38		50	69	70	85	
Matrix Position	0	1	2	3	4	5	6	7	8	9

These values are again reassigned to the original matrix in a *fifo* manner.

04 08 21 23 23 38 50 53 69 70 85 88

Since no member of this list has more than two digits, the list is now sorted. Had there been more digits, this process would be repeated, one pass for each digit in the largest number.

Ten matrices are required for a radix sort, one for each digit. Since you would not know ahead of time the number of numbers to be placed into any one matrix, each matrix would have to be dimensioned to hold the total number of numbers being sorted. If you were to use a single double-subscripted matrix, the first subscript would have to be dimensioned to 10 (for the digits 0 through 9). The second subscript would have to be the number of numbers to be sorted.

Selection Sort

In the selection sort, the list is traversed to pick out the smallest value. This value is assigned to the first position in a new list. A value is then given to its former position larger than any other value in the list. The original list is then reexamined for its smallest value, which is then assigned to the next position in the new list. Again a very large value is assigned to the old position. This search-assign-reassign procedure is repeated until all the values in the old list have been moved into the new list. For an N-item list, N passes through the list are required for a complete sort. What follows is an example of a selection sort.

```
A[1]   6 –    6      6      6      6      6      6      6      6    B[1] 1
A[2]   2 –  * 2 –  * 2 –  * 2 –  * 2 –  * 2 –  * 2 –    2      2
A[3]   4      4 –    4      4      4      4      4      4      4
```

```
A[4]     8      8      8 −    8      8      8      8      8      8
A[5]     9      9      9      9 −    9      9      9      9      9
A[6]     6      6      6      6      6 −    6      6      6      6
A[7]     5      5      5      5      5      5 −    5      5      5
A[8]     1      1      1      1      1      1      1 −  * 1 −  * 1 −  *
A[9]     3      3      3      3      3      3      3      3 −    3
A[10]    7      7      7      7      7      7      7      7      7 −


A[1]     6 −    6      6      6      6      6      6      6      6     B[1] 1
A[2]     2 −  * 2 −  * 2 −  * 2 −  * 2 −  * 2 −  * 2 −  * 2 −  * 2 −  *B[2] 2
A[3]     4      4 −    4      4      4      4      4      4      4
A[4]     8      8      8 −    8      8      8      8      8      8
A[5]     9      9      9      9 −    9      9      9      9      9
A[6]     6      6      6      6      6 −    6      6      6      6
A[7]     5      5      5      5      5      5 −    5      5      5
A[8]   999    999    999    999    999    999    999 −  999    999
A[9]     3      3      3      3      3      3      3      3 −    3
A[10]    7      7      7      7      7      7      7      7      7 −


A[1]     6 −  * 6 −    6      6      6      6      6      6      6     B[1] 1
A[2]   999 −  999    999    999    999    999    999    999    999    B[2] 2
A[3]     4      4 −  * 4 −  * 4 −  * 4 −  * 4 −  * 4 −  * 4 −    4     B[3] 3
A[4]     8      8      8 −    8      8      8      8      8      8
A[5]     9      9      9      9 −    9      9      9      9      9
A[6]     6      6      6      6      6 −    6      6      6      6
A[7]     5      5      5      5      5      5 −    5      5      5
A[8]   999    999    999    999    999    999    999 −  999    999
A[9]     3      3      3      3      3      3      3      3 −  * 3 −  *
A[10]    7      7      7      7      7      7      7      7      7 −


A[1]     6 −  * 6 −    6      6      6      6      6      6      6     B[1] 1
A[2]   999 −  999    999    999    999    999    999    999    999    B[2] 2
A[3]     4      4 −  * 4 −  * 4 −  * 4 −  * 4 −  * 4 −  * 4 −  * 4 −  *B[3] 3
A[4]     8      8      8 −    8      8      8      8      8      8     B[4] 4
A[5]     9      9      9      9 −    9      9      9      9      9
A[6]     6      6      6      6      6 −    6      6      6      6
A[7]     5      5      5      5      5      5 −    5      5      5
A[8]   999    999    999    999    999    999    999 −  999    999
A[9]   999    999    999    999    999    999    999    999 −  999
A[10]    7      7      7      7      7      7      7      7      7


A[1]     6 −  * 6 −  * 6 −  * 6 −  * 6 −  * 6 −    6      6      6     B[1] 1
A[2]   999 −  999    999    999    999    999    999    999    999    B[2] 2
A[3]   999    999 −  999    999    999    999    999    999    999    B[3] 3
```

```
A[4]     8      8      8 −     8      8      8      8      8      8      B[4] 4
A[5]     9      9      9      9 −     9      9      9      9      9      B[5] 5
A[6]     6      6      6      6      6 −     6      6      6      6
A[7]     5      5      5      5      5      5 −  * 5 −  * 5 −  * 5 −  *
A[8]    999    999    999    999    999    999    999 −  999    999
A[9]    999    999    999    999    999    999    999    999 −  999
A[10]    7      7      7      7      7      7      7      7      7 −

A[1]     6 −  * 6 −  * 6 −  * 6 −  * 6 −  * 6 −  * 6 −  * 6 −  * 6 −  * B[1] 1
A[2]    999 −  999    999    999    999    999    999    999    999    B[2] 2
A[3]    999    999 −  999    999    999    999    999    999    999    B[3] 3
A[4]     8      8      8 −     8      8      8      8      8      8      B[4] 4
A[5]     9      9      9      9 −     9      9      9      9      9      B[5] 5
A[6]     6      6      6      6      6 −     6      6      6      6      B[6] 6
A[7]    999    999    999    999    999    999 −  999    999    999
A[8]    999    999    999    999    999    999    999 −  999    999
A[9]    999    999    999    999    999    999    999    999 −  999
A[10]    7      7      7      7      7      7      7      7      7 −

A[1]    999 − * 999 − * 999 −  999    999    999    999    999    999    B[1] 1
A[2]    999 −  999    999    999    999    999    999    999    999    B[2] 2
A[3]    999    999 −  999    999    999    999    999    999    999    B[3] 3
A[4]     8      8      8 −  * 8 −  * 8 −     8      8      8      8      B[4] 4
A[5]     9      9      9      9 −     9      9      9      9      9      B[5] 5
A[6]     6      6      6      6      6 −  * 6 −  * 6 −  * 6 −  * B[6] 6
A[7]    999    999    999    999    999    999 −  999    999    999    B[7] 6
A[8]    999    999    999    999    999    999    999 −  999    999
A[9]    999    999    999    999    999    999    999    999 −  999
A[10]    7      7      7      7      7      7      7      7      7 −

A[1]    999 − * 999 − * 999 −  999    999    999    999    999    999    B[1] 1
A[2]    999 −  999    999    999    999    999    999    999    999    B[2] 2
A[3]    999    999 −  999    999    999    999    999    999    999    B[3] 3
A[4]     8      8      8 −  * 8 −  * 8 −  * 8 −  * 8 −  * 8 −  B[4] 4
A[5]     9      9      9      9 −     9      9      9      9      9      B[5] 5
A[6]    999    999    999    999    999 −  999    999    999    999    B[6] 6
A[7]    999    999    999    999    999    999 −  999    999    999    B[7] 6
A[8]    999    999    999    999    999    999    999 −  999    999    B[8] 7
A[9]    999    999    999    999    999    999    999    999 −  999
A[10]    7      7      7      7      7      7      7      7      7 −  *

A[1]    999 − * 999 − * 999 −  999    999    999    999    999    999    B[1] 1
A[2]    999 −  999    999    999    999    999    999    999    999    B[2] 2
A[3]    999    999 −  999    999    999    999    999    999    999    B[3] 3
```

```
A[4]     8        8        8-  *  8-  *  8-  *  8-  *  8-  *  8-  *  8-   *B[4] 4
A[5]     9        9        9      9-     9      9      9      9      9     B[5] 5
A[6]    999      999      999    999    999-   999    999    999    999    B[6] 6
A[7]    999      999      999    999    999    999-   999    999    999    B[7] 6
A[8]    999      999      999    999    999    999    999-   999    999    B[8] 7
A[9]    999      999      999    999    999    999    999    999-   999    B[9] 8
A[10]   999      999      999    999    999    999    999    999    999-

A[1]   999- * 999- * 999- * 999-   999    999    999    999    999    B[1] 1
A[2]   999-   999    999    999    999    999    999    999    999    B[2] 2
A[3]   999    999-   999    999    999    999    999    999    999    B[3] 3
A[4]   999    999    999-   999    999    999    999    999    999    B[4] 4
A[5]    9      9      9      9-  *  9-  *  9-  *  9-  *  9-  *  9-   *B[5] 5
A[6]   999    999    999    999    999-   999    999    999    999    B[6] 6
A[7]   999    999    999    999    999    999-   999    999    999    B[7] 6
A[8]   999    999    999    999    999    999    999-   999    999    B[8] 7
A[9]   999    999    999    999    999    999    999    999-   999    B[9] 8
A[10]  999    999    999    999    999    999    999    999    999-   B[10] 9
```

Shell Sort

The shell sort is a variation of the pair exchange sort. However, it does not compare and possibly exchange the values of immediate neighbors. In the shell sort, elements some distance apart are compared.

The distance between the elements to be compared is usually determined by dividing the number of elements in the list (N) by two. In the example that follows, the list has 10 elements; hence, the pairs to be compared are 1:6, 2:7, 3:8, 4:9, and 5:10. The comparison between the pairs is made with any appropriate exchange of values.

```
A[1]     6 -    6      6         6        6        6
A[2]     2      2 -    2         2        2        2
A[3]     4      4      4 ┐       1        1        1
A[4]     8      8      8 │       8 ┐      3        3
A[5]     9      9      9 ├ S     9 │      9 ┐      7
A[6]     6 -    6      6 │       6 ├ S    6 │      6
A[7]     5      5 -    5 │       5 │      5 ├ S    5
A[8]     1      1      1 ┘       4 │      4 │      4
A[9]     3      3      3         3 ┘      8 │      8
A[10]    7      7      7         7 ┘      7 ┘      9
```

The distance between the elements to be compared is now halved, truncating the quotient to an integer. In our example, the distance is now two (5/2 = 2.5; TRUNC(2.5) = 2). So the pairs become 1:3, 2:4, 3:5, 4:6, 5:7, 6:8, 7:9, 8:10.

A[1]	6⌐	1	1	1	1	1	1 –
A[2]	2 ⊢S	2 –	2	2	2	2	2
A[3]	1⌐	6	6 –	6	6	6 –	5 –
A[4]	3	3 –	3	3 –	3	3	3
A[5]	7	7	7 –	7	7⌐	5 –	6
A[6]	6	6	6	6 –	6 ⊢S	6	6
A[7]	5	5	5	5	5⌐	7	7
A[8]	4	4	4	4	4	4	4
A[9]	8	8	8	8	8	8	8
A[10]	9	9	9	9	9	9	9

Since a switch involved an element that was deemed to be in the right orientation (for example, A[5] and A[7]), the procedure must backtrack to make sure that all the previous comparisons are still valid. The backtracking continues until no switchings occur. At that point, forward progress continues where it had left off.

A[1]	1	1	1	1	1	1	1
A[2]	2	2	2	2 –	2	2	2
A[3]	5	5	5	5	5	5	5
A[4]	3	3	3 –	3 –	3	3	3
A[5]	6 –	6	6	6	6	6	6
A[6]	6	6⌐	4 –	4	4	4	4
A[7]	7 –	7 ⊢S	7	7	7 –	7	7
A[8]	4	4⌐	6	6	6	6 –	6
A[9]	8	8	8	8	8 –	8	8
A[10]	9	9	9	9	9	9 –	9

The distance between elements being compared is halved again and the comparisons are made. This process of halving the distance and comparing is continued until the distance is one. In the previous example, the next halving results in a distance of one.

```
A[1]    1 –   1       1     1     1         1          1
A[2]    2 –   2 –     2     2     2         2          2
A[3]    5     5 –     5 –   3     3         3          3 –
A[4]    3     3       3 –   5 –   5         5 ┐        4 –
A[5]    6     6       6     6 –   6 ┐       4 ┘ ⊢S     5
A[6]    4     4       4     4     4 ┘ ⊢S    6          6
A[7]    7     7       7     7     7         7          7
A[8]    6     6       6     6     6         6          6
A[9]    8     8       8     8     8         8          8
A[10]   9     9       9     9     9         9          9

A[1]    1     1       1     1     1
A[2]    2     2       2     2     2
A[3]    3     3       3     3     3
A[4]    4     4       4     4     4
A[5]    5     5       5     5     5
A[6]    6 –   6       6 –   6     6
A[7]    7 –   7 ┐     6 –   6     6
A[8]    6     6 ┘ ⊢S  7     7 –   7
A[9]    8     8       8     8 –   8 –
A[10]   9     9       9     9     9 –
```

The number of passes through the list takes $\log_2 N$ for the shell sort.

Merge Sort

The merge sort involves the merger of two sorted lists into a third list. For the sake of discussion, let the lists to be sorted be arrays A and B. The combined list is array C.

This algorithm involves taking the first element of A and comparing it to the first in B. The smaller of the two is sent to C, taking position 1. The key of the "winning" array (that is, the array with the smaller element) now becomes the element in the second position. This new key is to be compared with the first element in the "losing" array. Again the smaller element of the two is moved into the next position in C. The key of the winning array is then moved and the process repeated. The comparisons and appropriate moves are made until all elements of either array A or array B have been assigned to array C. At this point, the remaining elements of the losing array are moved directly into array C.

The following illustrates the merge sort. The keys have been starred.

```
A[1]      2      *      C[1]        1
A[2]      4
A[3]      6
A[4]      8
A[5]      9

B[1]      1      *
B[2]      3
B[3]      5
B[4]      6
B[5]      7

A[1]      2      *      C[1]        1
A[2]      4             C[2]        2
A[3]      6
A[4]      8
A[5]      9

B[1]      1
B[2]      3      *
B[3]      5
B[4]      6
B[5]      7

A[1]      2             C[1]        1
A[2]      4      *      C[2]        2
A[3]      6             C[3]        3
A[4]      8
A[5]      9

B[1]      1
B[2]      3      *
B[3]      5
B[4]      6
B[5]      7

A[1]      2             C[1]        1
A[2]      4      *      C[2]        2
```

A[3]	6		C[3]	3
A[4]	8		C[4]	4
A[5]	9			

B[1]	1	
B[2]	3	
B[3]	5	*
B[4]	6	
B[5]	7	

A[1]	2		C[1]	1
A[2]	4		C[2]	2
A[3]	6	*	C[3]	3
A[4]	8		C[4]	4
A[5]	9		C[5]	5

B[1]	1	
B[2]	3	
B[3]	5	*
B[4]	6	
B[5]	7	

A[1]	2		C[1]	1
A[2]	4		C[2]	2
A[3]	6	*	C[3]	3
A[4]	8		C[4]	4
A[5]	9		C[5]	5
			C[6]	6

B[1]	1	
B[2]	3	
B[3]	5	
B[4]	6	*
B[5]	7	

A[1]	2	C[1]	1
A[2]	4	C[2]	2
A[3]	6	C[3]	3

A[4]	8	*	C[4]	4
A[5]	9		C[5]	5
			C[6]	6
B[1]	1		C[7]	6
B[2]	3			
B[3]	5			
B[4]	6	*		
B[5]	7			
A[1]	2		C[1]	1
A[2]	4		C[2]	2
A[3]	6		C[3]	3
A[4]	8	*	C[4]	4
A[5]	9		C[5]	5
			C[6]	6
B[1]	1		C[7]	6
B[2]	3		C[8]	7
B[3]	5			
B[4]	6			
B[5]	7	*		
A[1]	2		C[1]	1
A[2]	4		C[2]	2
A[3]	6		C[3]	3
A[4]	8	*	C[4]	4
A[5]	9		C[5]	5
			C[6]	6
B[1]	1		C[7]	6
B[2]	3		C[8]	7
B[3]	5		C[9]	8
B[4]	6			
B[5]	7	*		
A[1]	2		C[1]	1
A[2]	4		C[2]	2
A[3]	6		C[3]	3

A[4]	8		C[4]	4
A[5]	9	*	C[5]	5
			C[6]	6
B[1]	1		C[7]	6
B[2]	3		C[8]	7
B[3]	5		C[9]	8
B[4]	6		C[10]	9
B[5]	7			

In the worst case, the merge sort requires $N(\log_2(N/2))$ comparisons to sort N items.

Note that the merge sort illustrated above is sometimes referred to as a two-way merge sort. This is because two separate input lists are merged into a single output list.

EXERCISES

4–1. Among the various sorting algorithms, perhaps the bubble sort is the easiest to write, although it is not necessarily the best algorithm to use in all cases. Write the bubble sort algorithm.

4–2. In many cases, the most appropriate algorithm for sorting a list is the insertion sort. Write out this algorithm.

Using each of the following algorithms, write a program in Pascal to sort an array of 10 elements. The elements in the array should be sorted into ascending order. The initial values are to be integers read from the keyboard. Have the program write out the values in the sorted array in order.

4–3. Bubble (exchange) sort

4–4. Insertion sort

4–5. Pair exchange sort

4–6. Quicksort

4–7. Radix sort

4–8. Selection sort

4–9. Shell sort

4–10. Using the algorithm for the merge sort, combine two 10-element arrays, A and B, into a single, sorted array, C. Assume that arrays

A and B are already sorted. All the values for arrays A and B are real numbers and are stored in files named Alpha and Beta, respectively. The final sorted array, C, is to be placed into file Gamma.

4–11. In the worst case of a linear search, what is the number of comparisons that must be made? (n represents the number of items in the list to be searched.)

　　a. n/2

　　b. n

　　c. 2 * n

　　d. n * n

　　e. $\log_2 n$

4–12. In the worst case of a binary search, what is the number of comparisons that must be made? (n represents the number of items in the list to be searched.)

　　a. n/2

　　b. n

　　c. 2 * n

　　d. n * n

　　e. $\log_2 n$

4–13. What is the Big-Oh notation for a binary search of an n-item list?

　　a. O(n/2)

　　b. O(n)

　　c. O(2 * n)

　　d. O(n * n)

　　e. $O(\log_2 n)$

4–14. What is the Big-Oh notation for a linear search for an n-item list?

　　a. O(n/2)

　　b. O(n)

　　c. O(2 * n)

　　d. O(n * n)

　　e. $O(\log_2 n)$

　　Match the appropriate Big-Oh notation with the respective sorting or searching algorithm for an n-item list.

4-15. Binary search   1. $O(n \log_2 n)$

4-16. Linear search   2. $O(n * n)$

4-17. Merge sort   3. $O(n^{3/2})$

4-18. Quicksort   4. $O(n)$

4-19. Selection sort   5. $O(\log_2 n)$

SEARCHING

We have discussed various sorting algorithms. Once you have a sorted list, the next step involves searching the list for a particular item. There are several ways of performing a search.

Linear Searching

In a linear search, each item in the list is examined until the desired item is found, assuming that it is present. In the best case, the desired item would be at the head of the list. In the worst case, it would be the very last item in the list. However, in the average case, it would be halfway down the list. For a list containing N items, the number of required comparisons would be 1, N, and N/2, respectively.

A linear search does not require that the number of items to be searched be known. The search continues through the list until either a match is found, or you run out of data.

Binary Searching

A binary search is generally faster than a linear search. In a binary search, the ordered list is halved, with the item halfway down the list being compared to the desired value. If this mid-value is less than the desired value, the lower half of the list is then examined. Otherwise, the upper half of the list is examined.

Whichever half is to be examined is again divided into two smaller lists before the comparison is made. The less-than-greater-than test is repeated. Again, a portion of the list is examined to determine which possibly has the match.

Basically, then, the binary search involves dividing the sorted list into successively smaller lists until either a match is made, or until you run out of data. In an N-item list, in the best case, the desired item is located in the exact center of the list. In the worst case, it is located either at the very beginning or at the very end of the list. The best case, again, requires 1 comparison. However, in the worst case, only $\log_2 N$ comparisons need to be made.

The difference between N and $\log_2$ N comparisons is very great. For a list containing, say, 50000 items, a linear search requires 50000 comparisons in the worst case. However, a binary search requires only about 16 comparisons ($\log_2 (50000) = 16$). The following graph illustrates a comparison between linear and binary searching items. In examining the graph, keep in mind that as the number of comparisons goes up, so does the time for the search.

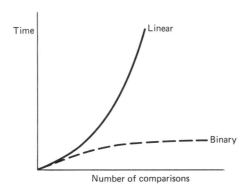

Number of comparisons

This is not to say that a binary searching algorithm is always preferred over a linear search. Two drawbacks to a binary search are that the number of items in the list must be known and that the list must be ordered initially. Without knowing the number of items in the list, you cannot determine where the center is. If the list is not ordered, it is impossible to determine which half of the list should be examined further. A linear search is not restricted by either of these factors.

ROUNDING ERRORS

Many people feel that in a discrepancy between a person and a computer, the computer is probably right—computers don't make mistakes. This is most certainly false. Computers do make mistakes. Many of the errors that computers do make arise from the manner in which a computer stores values, particularly numbers.

As was stated earlier in this book, computers store numbers as a sequence of binary digits, or bits. There is a limit on how many bits can be used to represent a number. Hence, there is a limit to the ultimate size of a number. This limitation pertains not only to integers but also to real numbers.

Real numbers are composed of two parts, a mantissa and an exponent. In the following example, the 0.1234 is the mantissa and the -17 is the exponent:

    0.1234E-17

Note that, unlike "proper" scientific or exponential notation, in floating-point notation there is no nonzero digit to the left of the decimal point. In floating-point notation, the digit to the left of the decimal point is always zero.

The number of digits in the mantissa is generally limited to six. Excess digits are lost. The manner in which these excess digits are lost varies from computer to computer. In some cases, they are just dropped, or truncated. In other cases, the number is rounded off to the proper number of digits.

In rounding, if the excess digits are greater than 0.000005 and the number is positive, then the last digit of the number is increased by 1.

    .123456 + .0000051 = .123457

If the number is negative, then 1 is subtracted from the last digit.

    − .123456 .0000051 = − .123455

You need to keep the problem of rounding error in mind when writing programs using very large or very small numbers (computing 1000! with absolute accuracy, for example).

EXERCISES

4–20. Which of the following Pascal expressions is equivalent to ROUND(X), when X is not negative?

   a. TRUNC(X + 1)
   b. TRUNC(X + 0.5)
   c. TRUNC(X)
   d. TRUNC(X − 0.5)
   e. TRUNC(X − 1)

4–21. What is the value of Answer after the following statement is executed?

   Answer := ROUND(1.5 + TRUNC(− 1.1111 * 9));

a. − 8

b. − 7

c. 10

d. 11

e. 12

4–22. Assume that the FUNCTION RandomNumber is a random number generator that returns a REAL value between 0 and 1, including 0 but excluding 1. Which of the following expressions returns a random number between 1 and 100, inclusive?

a. TRUNC(100 * RandomNumber)

b. ROUND(100 * RandomNumber)

c. TRUNC(100 * RandomNumber + 1)

d. ROUND(100 * RandomNumber + 1)

e. TRUNC(100 * (RandomNumber + 1))

4–23. When are TRUNC(Z2 + 0.5) and ROUND(Z2) equal, if Z is a REAL number?

a. All the time

b. Only when Z is positive

c. Only when Z is negative

d. Only when Z is positive or zero

e. Only when Z is a nonnegative integer

4–24. When are TRUNC(Z3 + 0.5) and ROUND(Z3) equal, if Z is a REAL number?

a. All the time

b. Only when Z is positive

c. Only when Z is negative

d. Only when Z is nonnegative

e. None of the above

4–25. $1,000 is put into a bank account, and it is compounded continually at an annual rate of 4 percent interest. The FUNCTION Money(Y) returns the amount of interest (to three decimal places) that has been compounded after Y years. Which of the following Pascal statements shows the number of dollars in the account after 15 years? (The banks round to the nearest penny.)

a. WRITELN (1000 + ROUND(Money(15)));
b. WRITELN (1000 + TRUNC(Money(15) + 0.5));
c. WRITELN (1000 + ROUND(Money(15) * 100));
d. WRITELN (1000 + TRUNC(Money(15) * 100));
e. WRITELN (1000 + ROUND(Money(15) * 100) / 100);

4–26. Which of the following expressions produces -3.4 as an answer?

a. ROUND(-3.4) + TRUNC(-3.4)
b. ROUND(-3.4) + ROUND(-4.3)
c. ROUND(-3.4) + ROUND(-3.4 / 10)
d. ROUND(-3.4) + TRUNC(-3.4 * 10) / 10
e. ROUND(-3.4) + ROUND(-4.3) / 10

4–27. Which of the following expressions rounds X to Y decimal places?

a. ROUND(Y / 10X) * 10X
b. ROUND(Y / 10(X + 1)) * 10(x + 1)
c. ROUND(Y * 10X) / 10X
d. ROUND(Y * 10(X + 1)) / 10(X + 1)
e. None of the above

4–28. When do ROUND(X) and TRUNC(X) return the same values, if X is positive?

a. Never
b. When X is less than or equal to 1
c. When the fractional part of X is less than 0.5
d. When the fractional part of X is less than or equal to 0.5
e. Always

4–29. Which of the following is true is X is any REAL number?

a. TRUNC(ROUND(X)) = ROUND(TRUNC(X))
b. TRUNC(ROUND(X)) = ROUND(TRUNC(X + 0.5))
c. TRUNC(ROUND(X + 0.5)) = ROUND(X)
d. TRUNC(X) = ROUND(TRUNC(X + 0.5))
e. None of the above

The following portion of a Pascal program is used in exercises 4–30 through 4–34.

PROGRAM Bisection; (* This program finds a root of the function f(x), defined below, by using the bisection method. *)

```
VAR
  LowerLimit, UpperLimit, Value, Error : REAL;
  Count : 0 .. 100;

FUNCTION f(x : REAL) : REAL;
  ...
  ...

BEGIN (* Bisection *)
  WRITE ('What is the allowable error ? ');
  READLN(Error);
  WRITE ('What are the lower and the upper limits ? ');
  READLN(LowerLimit, UpperLimit);
  Count := 0;
  REPEAT
    Value := (LowerLimit + UpperLimit) / 2;
  IF (f(Value) > 0)
    THEN LowerLimit := Value
    ELSE UpperLimit := Value;
  Count := Count + 1;
  IF (Count = 100)
    THEN
      BEGIN (* THEN loop *)
        WRITELN ('An approximation within ', Error, ' was not');
        WRITELN ('found after 100 passes through the loop.');
        Count := 0
      END; (* THEN loop *)
  UNTIL ((Count = 0) OR (UpperLimit − LowerLimit Error));
  IF (Count ⟩= 0)
    THEN
      BEGIN (* THEN loop *)
        WRITELN (Value, ' is within ', Error, ' of a root of the');
        WRITELN ('given function in ', Count, ' passes.')
      END (* THEN loop *)
END. (* Bisection *)
```

4–30. If the function f(X), above, is equal to (X − 5), the Error is typed in as 0.1, the lower limit as 0, and the upper limit as 10, how many passes through the loop will it make before it is done?

   a. 1

   b. 2

   c. 5

   d. 7

   e. 100, and it will not have found a root.

4–31. What is the programmer's main purpose in the *second* line that reads "Count := 0;"?

   a. It starts the loop over again if a zero to the function f(X) was not found with the first set of data.

   b. It terminates the program immediately.

   c. It acts as a flag to another part of the program.

   d. It is a completely optional line—it could be deleted without changing the operation of the program in any way.

   e. It is a way of resetting the variable Count so it doesn't exceed the subrange in which it is defined.

4–32. What happens if the lower and upper limits are typed into the computer in the wrong order—in other words, the UpperLimit is typed before the LowerLimit—assuming there actually is a root between the two values?

   a. The program's output appears to be normal, and the answer reported is correct.

   b. The program runs through the loop twice, then falls out and says a root could not be found within 100 tries.

   c. The program runs through the loop once and reports having found a root, but the root isn't actually between the numbers it reports.

   d. The program runs through the loop once and reports having found a root. The root is between the numbers it reports, but the numbers are more than Error away from each other.

   e. The program causes a run-time error.

4–33. What does the program do if no root is contained within the limits that are entered?

a. It runs through the loop once and then reports that it couldn't find a root.

b. It runs through the loop 100 times and then reports that it couldn't find a root.

c. It runs through the loop, only changing one of the two limits, until the difference between the two limits is less than Error. It then reports having found a root, even though one does not exist in the interval it reports.

d. It runs through the loop until the difference between the two limits is less than Error. It then reports finding no root.

e. The program eventually causes a run-time error or goes into an infinite loop.

4–34. For which of the following sets of input would the program correctly report having found a root in a small interval, if the function is as follows:

$$f(X) = X + 2$$

	Error	LowerLimit	UpperLimit
a.	0.01	−4	−3
b.	0.01	−1	−3
c.	0.01	0	1000000
d.	0.01	−1000000	1000000
e.	None of the above.		

5

Computer Applications

COMPUTER APPLICATIONS

Most people in society will not become computer programmers, but they will become computer users. The possible uses of computers in society are almost too numerous to comprehend. What follows is but a very brief list of these uses.

Word Processing

Before the advent of computers, whenever students had to write term papers, they had one of two choices: write it out or type it. Whichever method they chose, they always had difficulty altering the paper once it was completed. Today, with the word—processing capabilities of a computer, a term paper can be altered very easily, and with the press of a key, automatically retyped. Such was the case with the drafts of this book. The word processor saved me countless hours of retyping.

Word processors today are quite sophisticated. They allow for a check on spelling, including the spelling of a word in the context that it is used. Left and right justification are also possible. Add to this enhancements such as automatic page numbering, footnoting, and indexing, and you arrive at a very powerful tool. Most word processors have, as a minimum, the following abilities:

1. ASCII data file conversion
2. Creating a document
3. Deleting a document
4. Editing a document

5. Showing an index of the documents
6. List processing
7. Printing a document

Perhaps an explanation is warranted for the first and sixth functions.

The ASCII data file conversion utility allows you to take any ASCII file, be it a text file, a Pascal program, or whatever, and copy it into a word—processing document without having to retype it. With list processing, you can merge two or more documents into a new document without altering the original documents or you can selectively remove parts of one or more documents to form a new one. For example, in one document could be, say, a thousand multiple—choice questions dealing with chemistry, each coded with an indication as to its difficulty level. With list processing, the computer could randomly select, say, 100 of these questions, with so many chosen from each of the different levels. Another use of list processing might be to take a form letter from one document and the names and addresses of its intended recipients from another. Each recipient then would receive an individually addressed letter.

Simulation

With the increased number of space flights occurring today, we are tempted to forget all the work that goes into the preparation for these flights. Before any living creature is placed into a spaceship, computers are used to simulate the flight. Any errors or possible problems are determined and solved before these flights.

Simulation is used today in the training of airline pilots, the design of automobiles, and the design of roadways. The list is almost endless. On occasion, computer simulation is used to help us prepare for possible future events. The computer was used in the design of buildings in California so as to heighten their ability to withstand earthquakes of various magnitudes. Simulation plays a large part in the training of nuclear reactor operators.

Data Manipulation

Our space probes into the outer reaches of the Solar System and beyond have sent to the Earth millions upon millions of pieces of data. It would take many, many years to analyze this data. With computers, this time is cut drastically.

Once analyzed, data can be presented to the user in a variety of forms. These forms include tables, pie charts, bar graphs, and line graphs.

Each has its own strengths and weaknesses. Hence, in any one instance, one method of representation might be preferred over another.

Large amounts of data with corresponding analysis is but one problem that can be solved with computers. Another is the management of this data. How do you store massive amounts of data—on scraps of paper stored in filing cabinets? That is not too practical. You can store the information contained on approximately 200,000 pages of text in less than 0.5 cubic feet of space in a computer. As of this writing, technology is being developed to increase the amount of information that can be stored in this same space to more than one million pages.

Obviously, the concentration of such massive amounts of information creates many problems. How is the information to be retrieved? By whom? When? What happens if the information is lost? Is this information form legal?

Many departments of a business might wish to access a common data base instead of maintaining separate data bases. These items might be included in a single data base in a business:

1. name and address
2. telephone number (including unlisted ones)
3. Social Security number
4. what credit cards a person has
5. what a person's credit line is on each credit card
6. salary, including all sources of income
7. a past purchase history
8. bill payment history
9. employment history

Who can access what parts of the data base is a question that should concern us all.

Games

A number of computers were initially sold to people as an expensive form of entertainment. Some people felt that it would be better in the long run to buy their child a computer than to allow them to drop quarters into arcade machines. Besides, maybe they would eventually use the computer for nongame purposes, they theorized.

The games that initially came out for the personal computers were little more than arcade—type games. Little by little, this changed. The games became more educational in nature. Such games as the Towers of Hanoi and Tic—Tac—Toe were manufactured to help improve logic. Many shooting games were adapted for other purposes (for example, to teach touch typing).

Regardless of the intended application for the computer, it must have system software. System software is used to actually control the computer. Computers are stupid. Computers cannot think. They must be told how to do everything from controlling what goes onto the screen to checking the syntax of a program and from carrying out arithmetic operations to drawing a pie chart.

EXERCISES

The following portion of a Pascal program is referred to in exercises 5–1 through 5–4.

```
PROGRAM TowersOfHanoi (INPUT, OUTPUT);

  TYPE
    Range = 0 .. 15;

  VAR
    NumberOfDisks : Range;

  PROCEDURE Hanoi (Height, From, To, Ignoring : Range);
    BEGIN (* Hanoi *)
      IF (Height 0)
        THEN
          BEGIN (* THEN loop *)
            Hanoi (Height − 1, From, Ignoring, To);
            WRITELN ('Move block from peg', From, 'to peg', To);
            Hanoi (Height − 1, Ignoring, To, From)
          END (* THEN loop *)
    END; (* Hanoi *)
  BEGIN (* TowersOfHanoi *)
    WRITELN ('How many disks are to be used?');
    READLN(NumberOfDisks);
    Hanoi(NumberOfDisks, 1, 3, 2)
  END. (* TowersOfHanoi *)
```

5–1. How is the problem of moving a large pile of disks handled by this program?

a. The program runs in an infinite loop, except that it crashes after the proper number of steps have been executed. The crash is brought about by subtracting 1 from Height continually, as it is defined on a subrange of 0 to 15.

b. The program uses a recursive procedure to simplify the task each time it is called.

c. The program simply keeps running until Height = 0. Then it stops, because the proper number of calculations have been performed.

d. The program does not work, that is, it does not print a working solution to the Towers of Hanoi.

e. None of the above. That is, the program does work, but none of the previous methods is the one used by the program.

5–2. How many times is the procedure Hanoi invoked if the user types in 4 for the number of disks?

a. 3

b. 7

c. 15

d. 31

e. 63

5–3. For the same conditions as above, how many steps are output in the Answer to the tower problem?

a. 3

b. 7

c. 15

d. 31

e. 63

5–4. In the program above, which of the following changes could be made to the WRITELN inside the procedure Hanoi that would correctly report which disks were moved from where to where?

a. WRITELN('Move disk', Ignoring, 'from peg', From, 'to peg', To);

b. WRITELN('Move disk', From - To, 'from peg', From, 'to peg', To);

c. WRITELN('Move disk', To - From, 'from peg', From, 'to peg', To);

d. WRITELN('Move disk', Ignoring - (To + From), 'from peg', From, 'to peg', To);

e. None of the above

The following FUNCTION is referred to by exercises 5–5 through 5–7.

```
TYPE
  Pieces = (His, Mine, Unused);
  BoardType = PACKED ARRAY [1 .. 3, 1 .. 3] OF pieces;

FUNCTION TicTacToe (Board : BoardType) : BOOLEAN;

VAR
  Row, Column : 1 .. 3;
  Temp : BOOLEAN;

BEGIN (* TicTacToe *)
  TicTacToe := FALSE;
  FOR Row := 1 TO 3 DO
    BEGIN (* FOR loop *)
      Temp := TRUE;
      FOR Column := 1 TO 3 DO
        Temp := Temp AND (Board[Row][Column] = His);
      IF Temp
        THEN TicTacToe := Temp
    END; (* FOR loop *)
  FOR Column := 1 TO 3 DO
    BEGIN (* FOR loop *)
      Temp := TRUE;
      FOR Row := 1 TO 3 DO
        Temp := Temp AND (Board[Row][Column] = His);
      IF Temp
        THEN TicTacToe := Temp
    END; (* FOR loop *)
  Temp := TRUE;
  FOR Row := 1 TO 3 DO
    Temp := Temp AND (Board[Row][Row] = His);
  IF Temp
    THEN TicTacToe := Temp
END; (* TicTacToe *)
```

5–5. There are three main parts to this FUNCTION. In which order do they appear?

    a. Check for TicTacToe in a row, then a column, then diagonally.

    b. Check for TicTacToe in a column, then a row, then diagnoally.

    c. Check for TicTacToe along a diagonal, then in a row, then in a column.

    d. Check for TicTacToe along a diagonal, then in a column, then in a row.

    e. Check for TicTacToe in a row, then along a diagonal, then in a column.

5–6. Does this function completely check a TicTacToe board, or could it miss a TicTacToe? If so, where would this TicTacToe be?

    a. It checks the board completely. It doesn't miss any.

    b. It checks the board completely for rows and columns, but it might miss a diagonal since the variable Temp could have been reset previously.

    c. It checks the board completely for rows, but it might miss columns and/or diagonals, since the variable Temp may have been reset in the routine that checked for rows.

    d. It checks the board completely for diagonals, but it might miss rows and/or columns, as the variable Temp is reset by the routine that checks the diagonals, so it wouldn't necessarily hold its value throughout the entire FUNCTION.

    e. It checks the board completely for rows and columns, and it checks properly along one diagonal, but misses the other.

5–7. Why is the function TicTacToe set to FALSE in the first line of the FUNCTION?

    a. Because there is no TicTacToe at the beginning of a TicTacToe game. Thus, this is just an initialization routine used at the start of the game.

    b. Because the variable Temp gets its value as to whether there is a TicTacToe. And so, if TicTacToe is not defined, Temp would be undefined and would cause an error.

    c. Because the FUNCTION TicTacToe is never assigned a value unless there is a TicTacToe found in the routines that follow it. Thus, if no TicTacToe was found, the FUNCTION TicTacToe would be undefined unless this statement was here.

d. Because a FUNCTION must have a valid value throughout the entire execution of the main body of the FUNCTION. Otherwise, the FUNCTION would be undefined.

e. Because the FUNCTION would be undefined in the main program body unless it was given a definition immediately in the body of the FUNCTION, as the loops take too long, and the computer needs a value to work with back in the main body of the program long before the FUNCTION is actually finished executing.

6

Hardware

A basic computer usually consists of a keyboard, CPU, and monitor. The keyboard is the most common device used to enter information into the computer, be it data or a program. Likewise, the monitor is the most common device for information display. The CPU, or central processing unit, is the actual computer.

In addition to the keyboard, many computers are connected to either a cassette recorder, disk drive, or both. These devices, called peripherals, also aid in information manipulation. Data, including programs, may be stored with these devices over long periods of time. The tape in a cassette recorder is similar to that used when recording music. On the other hand, a disk drive uses a diskette. A diskette is similar to a record.

There are a few differences between a diskette and a record. Diskettes are generally 5.25 inches in diameter, smaller than most records. Some diskettes have diameters of 8 inches. The newest trend in diskettes seems to be to have a 3.5-inch diameter. In addition to a size differential, you can record or erase information from a diskette.

The amount of information that may be stored on a diskette varies not only with its size, but also with how many sides will be used. If a diskette is set up for one-sided use, it is said to be single-sided. The term double-sided is reserved for diskettes that may be read from or recorded onto both sides.

Not all single-sided diskettes have the same maximum amount of information stored on them. The same is true for double-sided diskettes. Diskettes today are either single- or double-density in nature. Approximately 80–100 K bytes of information may be recorded onto a single-sided, single-density 5.25-inch diskette, whereas a double-sided, double-density 5.25-inch diskette holds almost 400 K bytes of information.

Since diskettes may hold valuable information, they need to be protected from possible damage. The worst enemies for diskettes are heat, a magnetic field, and dirt. The normal range of temperatures that a diskette should be subjected to is namely 50–100 degrees Fahrenheit. Since information is retained on a diskette according to the arrangement of tiny magnetic particles on the diskette's surface, exposing a diskette to a magnetic field would disturb this arrangement and should be avoided. To cut down on the amount of dirt on a diskette, manufacturers of diskettes have decided to enclose them in envelopes. The envelopes are sealed on all sides and have a minimum of openings. The openings are few and have specific functions. These are:

1. *Write-protect notch.* This, if present, is located along the right side of the diskette as one looks down on it. It is usually square-shaped. The presence of this notch allows the user to record or erase information from the diskette. When the notch is missing or covered up, no changes may be made to the information on the diskette. Covering this notch helps to prevent accidental erasure of information.
2. *Timing holes.* These holes, about 0.25 inches in diameter, are used to aid the computer in locating information on the diskette.
3. *Centering hole.* This large hole is located in the center of the diskette. The hole is used to center the diskette in the disk drive, hence its name. Sometimes this hole is reinforced with support material. This reinforcement serves to lengthen the life of the diskette.
4. *I/O hole.* The I/O (input/output) hole is oval in shape and is present on both sides of the diskette, regardless of whether the diskette is single- or double-sided.

The monitor for the computer may have a monochrome display. By this is meant that only one color is displayed. Originally many computers used a white display on a black background. Today this has been expanded to include green or amber on a black background. Many people have found green or amber displays to be easier on their eyes as compared to a white display.

Monitors may also be colored. Color monitors cost more than the same sized monochrome display. Color monitors are either composite or RGB in nature. A composite color monitor receives its signal along a single cable. An RGB, or red-green-blue monitor takes its signal from three separate cables. Although more expensive, an RGB monitor gives truer colors than does a composite monitor.

An ordinary television can also be used as a monitor. However, since a TV takes a different kind of signal than that given off by a computer, an extra device is needed to use a TV with a computer. This device is called an RF modulator. The RF modulator converts a computer-generated signal into one that can be correctly interpreted by the TV. Unfortunately with the use of an RF modulator comes a few problems. Most notably an RF modulator causes a decrease in image quality. Also, using a TV generally decreases the number of columns that may be displayed on the screen at one time. Some computer programs display 80 columns on a regular monitor, but only 40 on a TV.

Among the many parts of a CPU, there are two that are most important. These are ROM and RAM. ROM, or read-only memory, contains information that cannot be changed by the user. In the ROM are located such items as the language BASIC and the DOS, or disk operating system.

The part of memory that can be altered by the user is RAM. The acronym RAM stands for random-access memory. The amount of RAM in a computer may vary from 1 K bytes to several megabytes. Generally speaking, having more RAM available increases the maximum amount of information that may be stored in the CPU. I say generally speaking because there is a limit as to how much memory may be accessed by a CPU. This limit has to do with the number of address lines in the CPU. The maximum memory for a computer may be calculated by raising 2 (the number of possible states of a bit - 0 and 1) to a power equal to the number of address lines. The Intel 8088 CPU has 20 address lines, hence a computer that uses the 8088 has a maximum memory of approximately 1 megabyte ($2\hat{~}20$).

In reality not all addresses may be used freely. Some are reserved for special functions, for example, graphics. This serves to limit most personal computers to about 2/3 of this maximum memory size. 650 K bytes of RAM is a lot of memory (for an 8088-based computer). Because of the speed of access (as little as 200 nanoseconds), using RAM to execute programs is much preferred over disk drives. However, when insufficient RAM is available, large programs must be split into several parts, and accessed from the disk in order to be used.

Computers are used for rapid communication. There are basically two ways of communicating with a computer: parallel and serial. A parallel connection, or port, sends each of the 8 bits in a byte along a separate wire. In contrast to this, through a serial port all 8 bits are sent down the same wire.

A parallel port is less expensive than a serial one, but a parallel line longer than 20-30 feet may result in problems. In contrast, a serial port may make use of a line some 1500 feet in length.

The standard for serial communications is the RS-232-C. This standard was set forth by the Electronics Industries Association (EIA). For this reason, the RS-232-C is sometimes referred to as an EIA connection. Unfortunately the RS-232-C is not adhered to closely by all manufacturers of computers and peripherals. When buying two EIA peripherals, there is the possibility that their accompanying cables are not interchangeable.

EXERCISES

The following applies to questions 6-1 through 6-5:

    I RAM
    II ROM
    III Magnetic tape
    IV Floppy disk
    V Hard disk

6-1. Which of the above storage media would be best suited for use in archiving?

    a. I
    b. II
    c. III
    d. IV
    e. V

6-2. Which of the above storage media is fastest for storage/retrieval of data?

    a. I
    b. II
    c. III
    d. IV
    e. V

6-3. Which of the above media is most common in the microcomputer field for mass data storage?

    a. I
    b. II
    c. III
    d. IV
    e. V

6-4. Most computers have some sort of what is called 'scratch-pad' memory. Which of the above types of media is used for scratch-pad?

    a. I only

    b. I and II

    c. II only

    d. III only

    e. IV and/or V

6-5. Which of the above media use a magnetic storage method?

    a. I, II, and III

    b. II and III

    c. III only

    d. III and IV

    e. III, IV, and V

6-6. Most types of memory are measured in K, or kilobytes. A kilobyte is 1024 bytes. Which of the following is a typical amount of memory for a floppy disk?

    a. 0.4 K

    b. 4 K

    c. 40 K

    d. 400 K

    e. 4000 K

6-7. What is a megabyte?

    a. 10^6 bytes

    b. 2^6 bytes

    c. 2^{10} bytes

    d. 2^{16} bytes

    e. 2^{20} bytes

Bibliography

The following books might be helpful to someone preparing to take the Advanced Placement Computer Science Exam. Many of the books deal with the programming language Pascal. But remember, the Advanced Placement Program in Computer Science is not just a course in Pascal.

Aho, Alfred V., John E. Hopcroft, and Jeffrey D. Ullman. *Data Structures and Algorithms.* Reading, MA: Addison-Wesley Publishing Company, 1983.

Atkinson, L. V., and P. J. Harley. *An Introduction to Numerical Methods with Pascal.* Reading, MA: Addison-Wesley Publishing Company, 1983.

Barnes, J. G. P. *Programming in ADA.* Reading, MA: Addison-Wesley Publishing Company, 1982.

Carberry, M. S., H. M. Khalil, J. F. Leathrum, and L. S. Leavy. *Foundations of Computer Science.* Rockville, MD: Computer Science Press, 1979.

Chirlian, Paul M. *Pascal.* Beaverton, OR: Matrix Publishers, Inc. 1980

Clark, Randy, and Stephen Koehler. *The UCSD Pascal Handbook.* Englewood Cliffs, NJ: Prentice-Hall, Inc., 1982.

Conway, Richard, David Gries, and E. Carl Zimmerman. *A Primer on Pascal.* Second Edition. Boston: Little, Brown and Company, 1981.

Cooper, Doug, and Michael Clancy. *Oh! Pascal!.* New York: W. W. Norton & Company, 1982.

Dagless, Erik L., and David Aspinall. *Introduction to Microcomputers.* Rockville, MD: Computer Science Press, 1982.

Dale, Nell, and David Orshalick. *Introduction to Pascal and Structured Design.* Lexington, MA: D. C. Heath and Company, 1983.

Eisenbach, S., and C. Sadler. *Pascal for Programmers.* New York: Springer-Verlag, 1981.

Findlay, W., and D. A. Watt. *Pascal: An Introduction to Methodical Programming.* Rockville, MD: Computer Science Press, 1981.

Graybeal, Wayne, and Udo W. Pooch. *Simulation: Principles and Methods.* Cambridge, MA: Winthrop Publishers, Inc., 1980.

Grogono, Peter. *Programming in Pascal.* Second Edition. Reading, MA: Addison-Wesley Publishing Company, 1984.

Heller, Rachelle S., and C. Dianne Martin. *Bits 'n Bytes About Computing: A Computer Literacy Primer.* Rockville, MD: Computer Science Press, 1982.

Hergert, Richard, and Douglas Hergert. *Doing Business with Pascal.* Berkeley, CA: Sybex, Inc., 1983.

Holt, R. C., and J. N. P. Hume. *Programming Standard Pascal.* Reston, VA: Reston Publishing Company, Inc., 1980.

Hughes, Charles, Charles P. Pfleeger, and Lawrence L. Rose. *Advanced Programming Techniques: A Second Course in Programming Using FORTRAN.* New York: John Wiley & Sons, 1978.

Jensen, Kathleen, and Niklaus Wirth. *Pascal: User Manual and Report.* New York: Springer-Verlag, 1978.

Jones, William B. *Programming Concepts: A Second Course (with examples in Pascal).* Englewood Cliffs, NJ: Prentice-Hall, Inc., 1982.

Keller, Arthur M. *A First Course in Computer Programming.* New York: McGraw-Hill Book Company, 1982.

Kennedy, Michael, and Martin B. Solomon. *Pascal: Program Development With Ten Instruction Pascal Subsets (TIPS) and Standard Pascal.* Englewood Cliffs, NJ: Prentice-Hall, Inc., 1982.

Kernighan, Brian W., and P. J. Plauger. *Software Tools in Pascal.* Reading, MA: Addison-Wesley Publishing Company, 1981.

Koffman, Elliot B. *Problem Solving and Structured Programming in Pascal.* Reading, MA: Addison-Wesley Publishing Company, 1981.

——, **and Frank L. Friedman.** *Problem Solving and Structured Programming in BASIC.* Reading, MA: Addison-Wesley Publishing Company, 1979.

Knuth, Donald E. *The Art of Computer Programming. Vol. 1: Fundamental Algorithms.* Second Edition. Reading, MA: Addison-Wesley Publishing Company, 1973.

——. *The Art of Computer Programming. Vol. 2: Seminumerical Algorithms.* Second Edition. Reading, MA: Addison-Wesley Publishing Company, 1981.

——. *The Art of Computer Programming. Vol. 3: Sorting and Searching.* Reading, MA: Addison-Wesley Publishing Company, 1973.

Ledgard, Henry F., Paul A. Nagin, and John F. Hueras. *Pascal With Style.* Hasbrouck Heights, NJ: Hayden Book Company, Inc. 1979.

————, **and Andrew Singer.** *Elementary Pascal.* New York: Vintage Books, 1982.

Lightfoot, David. *Computer Programming in Pascal.* Kent, England: Hodder and Stoughton Ltd., 1983.

Lines, Vardell. *Pascal as a Second Language.* Englewood Cliffs, NJ: Prentice-Hall, Inc., 1984.

Logsdon, Tom. *Computers & Social Controversy.* Rockville, MD: Computer Science Press, 1980.

Lorin, Harold. *Sorting and Sort Systems.* Reading, MA: Addison-Wesley Publishing Company, 1975.

Luehrmann, Arthur, and Herbert Peckham. *Apple Pascal: A Hands-On Approach.* New York: McGraw-Hill Book Company, 1981.

Mazlack, Lawrence. *Structured Problem Solving With Pascal.* New York: Holt, Rinehart and Winston, 1983.

McGlynn, Daniel R. *Fundamentals of Microcomputer Programming, Including Pascal.* New York: John Wiley & Sons, Inc., 1982.

McGregor, James J., and Alan H. Watt. *Simple Pascal.* Rockville, MD: Computer Science Press, 1981.

Pattis, Richard E. *Karel The Robot: A Gentle Introduction to the Art of Programming.* New York: John Wiley & Sons, 1981.

Pohl, Ira, and Alan Shaw. *The Nature of Computation: An Introduction to Computer Science.* Rockville, MD: Computer Science Press, 1981.

Pratt, Terrence W. *Programming Languages: Design and Implementation.* Englewood Cliffs, NJ: Prentice-Hall, Inc., 1984.

Price, David. *Pascal: A Considerate Approach.* Englewood Cliffs, NJ: Prentice-Hall, Inc., 1982.

Ralston, Anthony, and Chester L. Meek (Editors). *Encyclopedia of Computer Science.* First Edition. New York: Van Nostrand Reinhold Company, 1976.

Richards, James L. *Pascal.* New York: Academic Press, 1982.

Sand, Paul A. *Advanced Pascal Programming Techniques.* Berkeley, CA: Osborne/McGraw-Hill, 1984.

Schneider, G. M., and S. C. Bruell. *Advanced Programming and Problem Solving With Pascal.* New York: John Wiley & Sons, 1981.

————, **Steven W. Weingart, and David M. Perlman.** *An Introduction to Programming and Problem Solving With Pascal.* Second Edition. New York: John Wiley & Sons, 1982.

Tenenbaum, Aaron M., and Moshe J. Augenstein. *Data Structures Using Pascal.* Englewood Cliffs, NJ: Prentice-Hall, Inc. 1981.

Tennent, R. D. *Principles of Programming Languages.* Englewood Cliffs, NJ: Prentice-Hall, Inc., 1981.

Tiberghien, Jacques. *The Pascal Handbook.* Berkeley, CA: Sybex, Inc., 1981.

Tomek, Ivan. *Introduction to Computer Organization.* Rockville, MD: Computer Science Press, 1981.

————. *The First Book of Josef: An Introduction to Computer Programming.* Englewood Cliffs, NJ: Prentice-Hall, Inc., 1983.

Tremblay, Jean-Paul, and Richard B. Bunt. *An Introduction to Computer Science: An Algorithmic Approach.* New York: McGraw-Hill Book Company, 1979.

————, and ————. *Instructor's Manual, An Introduction to Computer Science: An Algorithmic Approach.* New York: McGraw-Hill Book Company, 1979.

————, ————, and Lyle M. Opseth. *Structured Pascal.* New York: McGraw-Hill Book Company, 1980.

Tucker, Allen B., Jr. *Apple Pascal: A Programmer's Guide.* New York: Holt, Rinehart and Winston, 1982.

Wilson, I. R., and A. M. Addyman. *A Practical Introduction to Pascal.* New York: Springer-Verlag, 1981.

Wirth, Niklaus. *Systematic Programming: An Introduction.* Englewood Cliffs, NJ: Prentice-Hall, Inc., 1973.

————. *Algorithms + Data Structures = Programs.* Englewood Cliffs, NJ: Prentice-Hall, Inc., 1976.

Wulf, William A., Mary Shaw, Paul N. Hilfinger, and Lawrence Flon. *Fundamental Structures of Computer Science.* Reading, MA: Addison-Wesley Publishing Company, 1980.

Yourdon, Edward. *Writings of the Revolution.* New York: Yourdon Press, 1982.

Zwass, Vladimir. *Introduction to Computer Science.* New York: Barnes & Noble Books, 1981.

Appendix

Topical Outline for
Advanced Placement Computer Science

A. *Programming Methodology*
  1. Specification
     a. Problem definition and requirements
     b. Functional specifications for programs

  2. Design
     a. Modularization
     b. Top-down versus bottom-up methodologies
     c. Stepwise refinement of modules and data structures

  3. Coding
     a. Structure
     b. Style, clarity of expression

  4. Program correctness
     a. Testing
        1. Relation to design and coding
        2. Generation of test data
        3. Top-down versus bottom-up testing of modules
     b. Verification
        1. Assertions and invariants
        2. Reasoning about programs
     c. Debugging

  5. Documentation

B. *Features of Programming Languages*
   1. Types and declarations
      a. Block structures
      b. Scope of identifiers
         1. Local identifiers
         2. Global identifiers
   2. Data
      a. Constants
      b. Variables
   3. Expressions and assignments
      a. Operators and operator precedence
      b. Standard functions
      c. Assignment statements
   4. Control structures
      a. Sequential execution
      b. Conditional execution
      c. Assignment statements
   5. Input and output
      a. Terminal input and output
      b. File input and output
   6. Procedures
      a. Subroutines and functions
      b. Parameters
         1. Actual and formal parameters
         2. Value and reference parameters
      c. Recursive procedures
   7. Program annotation
      a. Comments
      b. Indentation and formatting

C. *Data Types and Structures*
   1. Primitive data types
      a. Numeric data
         1. Floating-point real numbers
         2. Integers
      b. Character (symbolic) data
      c. Logical (Boolean) data
   2. Linear data structures
      a. Arrays
      b. Strings
      c. Linked lists

      d. Stacks
      e. Queues

  3. Tree structures
     a. Terminology
       1. Nodes: root, leaf, parent, child, sibling
       2. Branches and subtrees
       3. Ordered and unordered trees
     b. Binary trees
     c. General tree structures (optional)

  4. Representation of data structures
     a. Sequential representation of linear structures
     b. Pointers and linked data structures

D. *Algorithms*
  1. Classes of algorithms
     a. Sequential algorithms
     b. Iterative or enumerative algorithms
     c. Recursive algorithms

  2. Searching
     a. Sequential (linear) search
     b. Binary search
     c. Hash-coded search
     d. Searching an ordered binary tree
     e. Linear versus logarithmic searching times

  3. Sorting
     a. Selection sort
     b. Insertion sort
     c. Exchange or bubble sort
     d. Merge sort
     e. Sorting using an ordered binary tree
     f. Quicksort (optional)
     g. Radix sort (optional)
     h. Quadratic vs. $n*\log(n)$ sorting times

  4. Numerical algorithms
     a. Approximations
       1. Zeros of functions by bisections
       2. Monte Carlo techniques
       3. Area under a curve (optional)
     b. Statistical algorithms
       1. Measures of central tendency
       2. Measures of dispersion

  c. Numerical accuracy
   1. Round-off effects
   2. Precision of approximations

 5. Manipulation of data structures
  a. String processing
   1. Concatenation
   2. Substring extraction
   3. Matching
  b. Insertion and deletion in linear structures, trees
  c. Tree traversals

E. *Applications of Computing*
 1. Text processing
  a. Editors
  b. Text formatters

 2. Simulation and modeling
  a. Continuous simulation of physical processes
  b. Discrete simulation of probabilistic events

 3. Data analysis
  a. Statistical packages
  b. Graphical display of data

 4. Data management
  a. Information storage and retrieval
  b. Typical business systems

 5. System software and graphics
  a. File-management routines (for example, mail systems)
  b. Syntax-analysis routines
   1. Command scanners
   2. Evaluation of arithmetic expressions
  c. Graphical software

 6. Games
  a. Simple puzzles (for example, Towers of Hanoi)
  b. Simple games (for example, Tic-Tac-Toe)
  c. Searching game trees (optional)

F. *Computer Systems*
 1. Major hardware components
  a. Primary and secondary memory
  b. Processors
  c. Peripherals

2. System software
    a. Language processors
    b. Operating systems
    c. Graphical output facilities
3. System configuration
    a. Microprocessor systems
    b. Time-sharing and batch-processing systems
    c. Networks
G. *Social Implications*
    1. Responsible use of computer systems
    2. Social ramifications of computer applications
        a. Privacy
        b. Values implicit in the construction of systems
        c. Reliability of systems

Note: Thorough coverage of topics E, F, and G require more time than is available in a single course. In an AP computer science course, a minimum treatment of these topics consists of the following. For topic E, simple examples of the applications listed in the topic outline should be studied in order to acquaint students with the general nature of these applications and to introduce students to the data structures and algorithms inherent in these applications. For topic F, a working knowledge of the major hardware and software components of a computer system should be developed, although the operation of these components need not be studied in detail. For topic G, the importance of considering the ethical and social implications of computing systems should be stressed throughout the course, although no systematic coverage of these implications is required. *

Reserved Words in ISO Standard Pascal

and	downto	if	or	then
array	else	in	packed	to
begin	end	label	procedure	type
case	file	mod	program	until
const	for	nil	record	var
div	function	not	repeat	while
do	goto	of	set	with

*Reprinted with permission from *Advanced Placement Course Description in Computer Science*, © 1984 by the College Entrance Examination Board, New York.

Predefined Identifiers in ISO Standard

Constants	*Functions*	*Procedures*
false	abs	dispose
maxint	arctan	get
true	chr	new
	cos	pack
Types	eof	page
boolean	eoln	put
char	exp	read
integer	ln	readln
real	odd	reset
text	ord	rewrite
	pred	unpack
Variables	round	write
input	sin	writeln
output	sqr	
	sqrt	
	succ	
	trunc	

Reserved Words in Standard UCSD Pascal

and	else	if	or	then
array	end	in	packed	to
begin	file	label	procedure	type
case	for	mod	program	until
const	forward	nil	record	var
div	function	not	repeat	while
do	goto	of	set	with
downto				

Non-UCSD-Pascal Standard Reserved Words in Apple Pascal

external
unit
interface
uses

segment
implementation

Predefined Identifiers in Apple Pascal

abs {r}	false {k}	maxint {k}	readln {p}	text {t}
blockread {i}	fillchar {p}	memavail {i}	real {t}	treesearch {i}
blockwrite {i}	get {p}	moveleft {p}	release {p}	true {k}
boolean {t}	gotoxy {p}	moveright {p}	reset {p}	trunc {i}
char {t}	halt {p}	new {p}	rewrite {p}	unitbusy {b}
chr {c}	input {f}	odd {b}	round {i}	unitclear {p}
close {p}	insert {p}	ord {i}	scan {i}	unitread {p}
concat {s}	integer {t}	output {f}	page {p}	seek {p}
copy {s}	interactive {t}	pos {i}	sizeof {i}	unitwait {p}
delete {p}	ioresult {i}	pred {−}	sqr {r}	unitwrite {p}
eof {b}	keyboard {f}	put {p}	str {s}	write {p}
eoln {b}	length {i}	pwroften {r}	string {t}	writeln {p}
exit {p}	mark {p}	read {p}	succ {−}	

{b} boolean function   {c} char function   {f} file
{i} integer function   {k} constant   {p} procedure
{r} real function   {s} string function   {t} type
{−} other

Nonstandard Reserved Words in OMSI Pascal

external
origin
forward
otherwise
nonpascal

Nonstandard Predefined Identifiers in OMSI Pascal

Functions	*Procedures*
bitsize	break
ref	close
size	seek
time	

Reserved Words in ADA

abort	delta	if	out	select
accept	digits	in	package	separate
access	do	is	pragma	subtype
all	else	limited	private	task
and	else if	loop	procedure	terminate
array	end	mod	raise	then
at	entry	new	range	type
begin	exception	not	record	use
body	exit	null	rem	when
case	for	of	renames	while
constant	function	or	return	with
declare	generic	others	reverse	xor
delay	goto			

Reserved Words in MODULA II

and	do	if	of	set
array	else	implementation	or	then
begin	elseif	import	pointer	to
by	end	in	procedure	type
case	exit	loop	qualified	until
const	export	mod	record	var
definition	for	module	repeat	while
div	from	not	return	with

Pascal Syntax Diagrams

⟨ARRAY_TYPE⟩ :

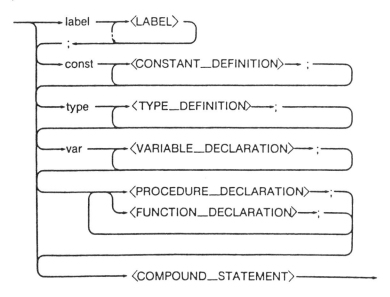

*except integer

⟨ASSIGNMENT_STATEMENT⟩:

⟨BLOCK⟩:

⟨CASE_STATEMENT⟩:

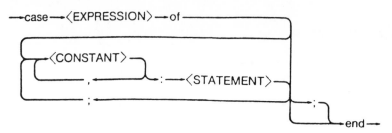

⟨CHARACTER_STRING⟩:

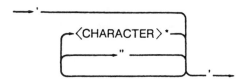

*The set of allowed characters is processor-dependent;
it does not include an apostrophe (').

⟨COMPOUND_STATEMENT⟩:

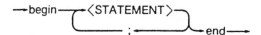

⟨CONSTANT⟩:

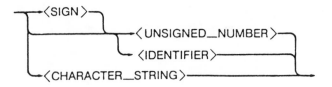

⟨CONSTANT_DEFINITION⟩:

—⟨IDENTIFIER⟩— = —⟨CONSTANT⟩——

⟨DIGIT⟩:

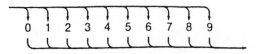

⟨DUMMY＿ARGUMENTS⟩:

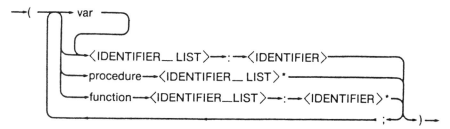

*Allows functions and procedures to be passed
as arguments.

⟨ENUMERATED＿TYPE⟩:

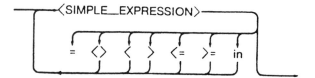

⟨EXPRESSION⟩:

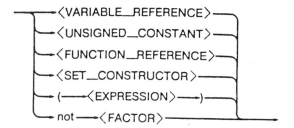

⟨FACTOR⟩:

                ⟨VARIABLE＿REFERENCE⟩
                ⟨UNSIGNED＿CONSTANT⟩
                ⟨FUNCTION＿REFERENCE⟩
                ⟨SET＿CONSTRUCTOR⟩
                (——⟨EXPRESSION⟩——)
                not ——⟨FACTOR⟩

⟨FILE＿TYPE⟩:

            file of ——⟨TYPE＿DENOTER⟩

⟨FOR_STATEMENT⟩:

—for—⟨IDENTIFIER⟩—:=—⟨EXPRESSION⟩—
—to—
—downto——⟨EXPRESSION⟩—do—⟨STATEMENT⟩—

⟨FUNCTION_ DECLARATION⟩:

—⟨FUNCTION_ HEADING⟩—; —⟨BLOCK⟩—

⟨FUNCTION_REFERENCE⟩:

—⟨IDENTIFIER⟩—
(—⟨EXPRESSION⟩—
,—)—

⟨FUNCTION_ HEADING⟩:

—function—⟨IDENTIFIER⟩—
—⟨DUMMY_ ARGUMENTS⟩—

⟨GOTO_STATEMENT⟩:

—goto—⟨LABEL⟩—

⟨IDENTIFIER⟩:

—⟨LETTER⟩—
—⟨DIGIT⟩—

⟨IDENTIFIER_LIST⟩:

—⟨IDENTIFIER⟩—
,

⟨IF—STATEMENT⟩:

→ if —⟨EXPRESSION⟩— then —⟨STATEMENT⟩—

— else —⟨STATEMENT⟩—

⟨LABEL⟩:

→⟨DIGIT⟩—

⟨LETTER⟩:

a b c d e f g h i j k l m n o p q r s t u v w x y z

⟨ORDINAL—TYPE⟩ :

— integer —
— boolean —
— char —
— ⟨ENUMERATED—TYPE⟩ —
— ⟨SUBRANGE—TYPE⟩ —
— ⟨IDENTIFIER⟩ —

⟨POINTER—TYPE⟩:

— ^ —
—⟨IDENTIFIER⟩—

⟨PROCEDURE—CALL⟩:

—⟨IDENTIFIER⟩—
(—⟨EXPRESSION⟩—
,)

⟨PROCEDURE_ DECLARATION⟩:

—→⟨PROCEDURE_ HEADING⟩—→ ; —→⟨BLOCK⟩—————→

⟨PROCEDURE_ HEADING⟩:

————→procedure ——→⟨IDENTIFIER⟩—┐
        └—⟨DUMMY_ ARGUMENTS⟩———┘—→

⟨PROGRAM⟩:

————————→program ——→⟨IDENTIFIER⟩—┐
     └—(—→⟨IDENTIFIER_LIST⟩ —→) —┐
         └— ; —→⟨BLOCK⟩————————→ ————→

⟨RECORD_TYPE⟩:

—————→record —┐
      ├————→⟨IDENTIFIER_ LIST⟩—→: —→⟨TYPE_ DENOTER⟩—┐
      │   ; ————————┘
      ├————→⟨VARIANT_PART⟩ ——————— ; ——┐
      └————————————————————— end ——→

⟨REPEAT_STATEMENT⟩:

—→repeat ——→⟨STATEMENT⟩—┐
            ; ——┘
         └—until—→⟨EXPRESSION⟩———→

⟨SET_CONSTRUCTOR⟩ :

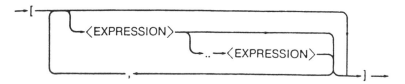

⟨SET_TYPE⟩:

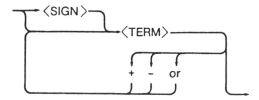

*except integer

⟨SIGN⟩ :

⟨SIMPLE_EXPRESSION⟩:

⟨STATEMENT⟩

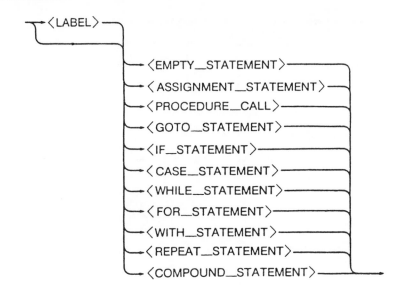

⟨STRUCTURED_TYPE⟩ :

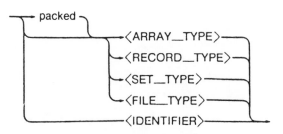

⟨SUBRANGE_TYPE⟩ :

⟶⟨CONSTANT⟩⟶.. ⟶⟨CONSTANT⟩⟶

⟨TERM⟩ :

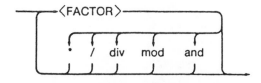

⟨TYPE__DEFINITION⟩:

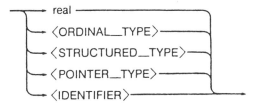

⟨TYPE__DENOTER⟩:

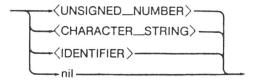

⟨UNSIGNED__CONSTANT⟩:

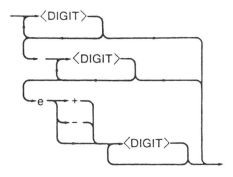

⟨UNSIGNED__NUMBER⟩:

⟨VARIABLE__ DECLARATION⟩:

→⟨IDENTIFIER__ LIST⟩→: →⟨TYPE__ DENOTER⟩→

⟨VARIABLE_REFERENCE⟩:

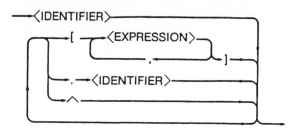

⟨WHILE_STATEMENT⟩:

⟨WITH_STATEMENT⟩:

—with—⟨IDENTIFIER⟩— , —do—⟨STATEMENT⟩—

Answers
to Exercises

CHAPTER 1 ANSWERS

1-1. True

1-2. B

1-3. E

1-4. C

1-5. A

1-6. A

1-7. B

1-8. D

1-9. C

1-10. D

CHAPTER 2 ANSWERS

2–1. Valid.

2–2. Valid.

2–3. Not valid. The dollar sign makes Name$ an invalid identifier. Identifiers must contain only alphanumeric characters.

2–4. Not valid. Ord is a reserved word, hence making it an invalid identifier.

2–5. Not valid. Although numerals may be contained within identifiers, the first character must be an alphabetic character.

2–6. Not valid. Standard Pascal does not allow for a hyphen in an identifier name.

2–7. Not valid. Identifier names must consist of only alphanumeric characters. This does not include a percent sign.

2–8. Not valid. Spaces are not allowed in identifier names.

2–9. Not valid. The apostrophe is not allowed in an identifier name. Only alphanumerics are allowed.

2–10. Not valid. Numeric characters are allowed in identifier names, but not as the first character.

2–11. Valid.

2–12. Valid.

2–13. REAL. Since the value of the identifier contains a decimal portion, a REAL identifier is needed.

2–14. CHAR. Since the value of the identifier is a literal, a CHAR identifier is needed (in particular, a PACKED ARRAY [1..4] OF CHAR).

2–15. INT. This numeric value does not have a decimal portion or even a decimal point. Hence an INT identifier is appropriate.

2–16. REAL. Although this value does not have a decimal portion, it does have a decimal point. Hence a REAL identifier is needed.

2–17. BOOLEAN. Assuming that the logical value FALSE is what is being specified, a BOOLEAN identifier is needed. If the literal False is what is being questioned, then a CHAR identifier (PACKED ARRAY [1..5] OF CHAR) is required.

2–18. CHAR. Since the value of the identifier is to be a literal, it must be of type CHAR. (See the answer for question 2–14.)

2–19. CHAR. A space is a valid value for an identifier. This is a literal; hence, an identifier of type CHAR is required. Since there is but a single space to be assigned to the identifier, a PACKED ARRAY is not needed.

2–20. REAL. The value of this division, namely 4.25, has a decimal portion, hence the REAL declaration.

2–21. CHAR. A literal needs to be assigned to a CHAR identifier, in this case, a PACKED ARRAY [1..18] OF CHAR identifier.

2–22. INT. The DIV type of division returns the integer portion of the quotient, in this case 4.

2–23. d. FifthVariable is local to procedure D and, hence, can only be accessed by procedure D.

2–24. a. Since FirstVariable is declared in program declaration section and not just in a specific procedure, it may be accessed throughout the program, regardless of the procedure in question.

2–25. c. SecondVariable, being declared in procedure A, is local to it. Hence it is accessible only in it. Since procedure B is nested in procedure A, SecondVariable may also be accessed in procedure B.

2–26. b. ThirdVariable is local to procedure B and, hence, can only be accessed by procedure B.

2–27. a. SixthVariable may be accessed only by procedure B, since it is declared only in that procedure.

2–28. e. FourthVariable is declared in procedure C. It may be accessed anywhere in that procedure, including any procedures that are nested therein (D and E, for example).

2–29. d. In nested procedures, the variables that may be accessed by the innermost nested procedure are: 1. those declared in that procedure (for example, FifthVariable), 2. those declared in the procedure in which the nesting occurs (for example, FourthVariable in procedure C), and 3. all global variables (for example, FirstVariable).

2–30. c. In a procedure, you may access: 1. all global variables (for example, FirstVariable), 2. any variables declared in that procedure (for example, ThirdVariable), and 3. if it is a nested procedure, any variables declared in the procedure(s) in which it is nested (for example, SecondVariable).

2–31. c. Procedures that are nested in other procedures must be so declared in the declaration section of the procedure in which the nesting occurs.

```
PROCEDURE C;
  VAR
    FourthVariable : INTEGER;
```

```
PROCEDURE D;
 VAR
   FifthVariable : CHAR;
 BEGIN (* procedure D *)

   ...
 END; (* procedure D *)
PROCEDURE E;
 VAR
   SixthVariable : CHAR;
 BEGIN (* procedure E *)

   ...
 END; (* procedure E *)
BEGIN (* procedure C *)

   ...
   D;

   ...
   E;

   ...
   E;

   ...
END; (* Procedure C *)
```

2–32. A. Global variables are declared in the declaration section of the program itself, not in a procedure (e.g., FirstVariable).

2–33. B. Procedures are executed sequentially, in the order in which they are called in the program.

2–34. A. PROCEDURE Fibonacci (Number : INTEGER);

```
VAR
  First, Second, Third, Counter : INTEGER;
  BEGIN (* Fibonacci *)
    First : = 1;
    Second : = 1;
    FOR Counter : = 1 TO Number DO
      BEGIN (* FOR loop *)
        Third : = First + Second;
        First : = Second;
        Second : = Third
      END; (* FOR loop *)
```

```
      WRITELN (Third)
   END; (* Fibonacci *)
```

B. PROCEDURE Fibonacci (Number : INTEGER);

```
   VAR
     First, Second, Third : INTEGER;

   PROCEDURE Fib (First, Second, Third, Number : INTEGER);

     BEGIN (* Fib *)
       Third : = First + Second;
       First : = Second;
       Second : = Third;
       IF Third 〈〉 Number
         THEN Fib (First, Second, Third, Number)
     END; (* Fib *)
   BEGIN (* Fibonacci *)
     First : = 1;
     Second : = 1;
     Fib (First, Second, Third, Number);
     WRITELN (Third)
   END. (* Fibonacci *)
```

2–35. PROCEDURE Factorial (Number : INTEGER);

```
   VAR
     First, Second : INTEGER;

   PROCEDURE Fact (First, Second, Number : INTEGER);

     BEGIN (* Fact *)
       First : = First + Second;
       Second : = Second + 1;
       IF Second 〈〉 Number
         THEN Fact (First, Second, Number)
     END; (* Fact *)

   BEGIN (* Factorial *)
     First : = 1;
     Second : = 1;
```

```
            Fact (First, Second, Number);
            WRITELN (First)
          END; (* Factorial *)
```

2–36. PROCEDURE Binary (Number : INTEGER);

```
        VAR
          FNumber : INTEGER;

        PROCEDURE Bin (FNumber, Number : INTEGER)

          BEGIN (* Bin *)
            FNumber := Number MOD 2;
            Number := Number DIV 2;
            Write (FNumber);
            IF Number <> 0
              TEN Bin (FNumber, Number)
          END; (* Bin *)

        BEGIN (* Binary *)
          FNumber := 1;
          Bin (FNumber, Number);
          WRITELN
        END; (* Binary *)
```

2–37. PROCEDURE Octal (Number : INTEGER);

```
        VAR
          FNumber : INTEGER;

        PROCEDURE Oct (FNumber, Number : INTEGER);

          BEGIN (* Oct *)
            FNumber := Number MOD 8;
            Number := Number DIV 8;
            WRITE (FNumber);
            IF Number <> 0
              THEN Oct (FNumber, Number)
          END; (* Oct *)
```

```
    BEGIN (* Octal *)
      FNumber := 1;
      Oct (FNumber, Number);
      WRITELN
    END; (* Octal *)
```

2–38. PROCEDURE Change (NUMBER, Base : INTEGER);

```
    VAR
      FNumber : INTEGER:

    PROCEDURE Ch (FnNumber, Number, Base : INTEGER);

      BEGIN (* Ch *)
        FNumber := Number MOD Base;
        Number := Number DIV Base;
        WRITE (FNumber);
        IF Number () 0
          THEN Ch (FNumber, Number, Base)
      END; (* Ch *)

    BEGIN (* Change *)
      FNumber := 1;
      Ch (FNumber, Number, Base);
      WRITELN
    END; (* Change *)
```

2–39. PROCEDURE SquareRoot (Number : REAL);

```
    VAR
      Flag : BOOLEAN;              (* signals a decimal point *)
      FirstNumber : REAL;          (* temporarily stored number *)
      Counter,                     (* used in a loop *)
      FirstCounter,                (* # of pairs of digits in # *)
      SecondCounter,               (* isolation of left digits *)
      SecondNumber,                (* divisor *)
      ThirdNumber : INTEGER;       (* left-most digits *)

    BEGIN (* SquareRoot *)
      Flag := FALSE;               (* initializes decimal-signal *)
```

```
        SecondNumber := 1;          (* initializes divisor *)
        FirstNumber := Number;      (* stores number *)
        FirstCounter := 0;          (* initializes number of pairs *)


    (* write a decimal point when needed *)
    IF (Number < 1) AND (Flag = FALSE)
        THEN
            BEGIN (* IF conditional *)
                WRITE ('.');
                FLAG := TRUE;
                Number := Number * 100
            END; (* IF conditional *)


(* determine the number of pairs of digits in number *)
WHILE (FirstNumber > 0) DO
    BEGIN (* WHILE LOOP *)
        FirstNumber := FirstNumber DIV 100;
        FirstCounter := FirstCounter + 1
    END; (* WHILE LOOP *)


(* isolates the first digit or two digits *)
SecondCounter := 1;
FOR Counter := 1 TO FirstCounter DO
    SecondCounter := SecondCounter + 1;


(* determine the digit in the quotient *)
SecondNumber := 1;
WHILE ThirdNumber DIV (SecondNumber * SecondNumber) > 0 DO
    SecondNumber := SecondNumber + 1;
WRITE (SecondNumber);


SecondNumber := SecondNumber * 20; (* determine divisor *)


(* set up next smaller number *)
Number := Number MOD SecondCounter;


IF Number > E-8
    THEN SquareRoot (Number) (* repeat if necessary *)


END; (* SquareRoot *)
```

2–40. 7 / 2 DIV 3 = 3.5 DIV 3 = 1

2–41. 4 * 3 + 2 − (7 + 3) MOD 3 = 4 * 3 + 2 − 10 MOD 3 = 12 + 2 − 1 = 13

2–42. 8 MOD (3 + 1) = 8 MOD 4 = 0

2–43. 7 DIV 2 = 3

2–44. 1 * 4 / 2 * 3 + 1 = 4 / 2 * 3 + 1 = 2 * 3 + 1 = 6 + 1 = 7

2–45. (5 / 9) * (98.6 − 32) = .555555 * 66.4 = 37

2–46. 37 * 9 / 5 + 32 = 333 / 5 + 32 = 66.6 + 32 = 98.6

2–47. 17 DIV 4 MOD 3 = 4 MOD 3 = 1

2–48. 4 + 2 * 3 / 4 = 4 + 6 / 4 = 4 + 1.5 = 5.5

2–49. 9 − 3 * 2 − (2 + 1) * 2 = 9 − 3 * 2 − 3 * 2 = 9 − 6 − 6 = − 3

2–50. 14

2–51. Error; Third is a REAL number, wheareas Temp2 is an INTEGER.

2–52. 5

2–53. 1

2–54. − 1

2–55. Error; ThirdParameter must be either REAL or INTEGER.

2–56. Error; FirstParameter must be of type INTEGER.

2–57. Error; SecondParameter must be of type CHAR.

2–58. REAL

2–59. BOOLEAN

2–60. CHAR

2–61. REAL

2–62. REAL

2–63. INTEGER

2–64. Error; ThirdParameter must be either REAL or INTEGER.

2–65. REAL

2–66. Error; FirstParameter must be the name of a FILE.

2–67. REAL

2–68. CHAR

2–69. REAL

2– 70. REAL

2–71. CHAR

2–72. SQRT(SQR(A) + SQR(B))

2–73. J := J + 2;

2–74. P := T * EXP(200 * LN(1 + X / T));

2–75. Y := M * X + B;

2–76. E := M * SQR(C);

2–77. CelsiusTemperature := (5 / 9) * (FahrenheitTemperature − 32);

2–78. HeatLost := Mass * ChangeInTemperature * SpecificHeat;

2–79. Author := 'John E. Parnell';

2–80. P := P − 100;

2–81. P1 := (V1 * P2 * (T1 + 273)) / ((T2 + 273) * V2);

2–82.   10

2–83.   1000

2–84.   100

2–85. infinite loop

2–86.   100

2–87.   1

                  2

                  3

                  .

                  .

                  .

               100

               100

2–88. IF HOURS ⟨= 12
      THEN WRITELN (Hours:1, ':', Minutes:1, ' A.M.')
      ELSE WRITELN ((Hours − 12):1, ':', Minutes:1, ' P.M.');

2–89.   CASE Month OF
   'JAN','MAR','MAY','JUL','AUG','OCT','DEC'
     : WRITELN (31:2, ' days');

```
            'APR','JUN','SEP','NOV' : WRITELN (30:2, ' days');
            'FEB' : WRITELN (28:2, ' days')
         END;

2–90.       IF NOT LeapYear
         THEN CASE Month OF
            'JAN','MAR','MAY','JUL','AUG','OCT','DEC'
              : WRITELN (31:2, ' days');
            'APR','JUN','SEP','NOV' : WRITELN (30:2, ' days');
            'FEB' : WRITELN (28:2, ' days')
         END
         ELSE CASE Month OF
            'JAN','MAR','MAY','JUL','AUG','OCT','DEC'
              : WRITELN (31:2, ' days');
            'APR','JUN','SEP','NOV' : WRITELN (30:2, ' days');
            'FEB' : WRITELN (29:2, ' days')
         END;
```

The answer to this question may be different than the above. Another answer might be to alter the last portion of the answer to question 2–89 to read

```
   'FEB' : IF NOT LeapYear
        THEN WRITELN (28:2, ' days')
        ELSE WRITELN (29:2, ' days')
```

```
2–91. FOR Interest := 5 TO 15 DO
        FOR Increment :=0 TO 9 DO
          BEGIN
            Annual := (Interest * 10 + Increment) / 1000;
            Yield := Deposit * Annual;
            WRITELN ('The interest earned is $', Yield:2:2)
          END;

2–92. Interest := 5;
      WHILE Interest ⟨ 16 DO
        BEGIN
          Increment := 0;
          WHILE Increment ⟨ 10 DO
            BEGIN
              Annual := (Interest * 10 + Increment) / 1000;
              Yield := Deposit * Annual;
              WRITELN ('The interest earned is $', Yield:2:2);
              Increment := Increment + 1
```

```
            END;
          Interest := Interest + 1
        END;


2-93.  Interest := 5;
       REPEAT
         Increment := 0;
         REPEAT
           Annual := (Interest * 10 + Increment) / 1000;
           Yield := Deposit * Annual;
           WRITELN ('The interest earned is $', Yield:2:2);
           Increment := Increment + 1
         UNTIL Increment = 9
       UNTIL Interest = 15;


2-94.  Number := 1;
       Power := 0;
       WHILE Number ⟨ 32767 DO
         BEGIN
           Number := Number * 2;
           Power := Power + 1
         END;


2-95.  Error := 0;
       Number := 1;
       WHILE Error = 0 DO
         Number := Number + 1;


2-96.  Week := Date DIV 7;
       Date := Date − Week * 7;
       CASE Date OF
           1 : Day := 'Tuesday';
           2 : Day := 'Wednesday';
           3 : Day := 'Thursday';
           4 : Day := 'Friday';
           5 : Day := 'Saturday';
           6 : Day := 'Sunday';
           7 : Day := 'Monday'
         END;


2-97.  FOR Person := 1 TO 50 DO
         WRITELN (Man[Person], '−', Woman[51 − Person]);
```

CHAPTER 3 ANSWERS

3–1. d. The percent signs cause the error.

3–2. e. The other answers all use colons, but in a TYPE definition, an equal sign is used.

3–3. a. A price needs to be a real number, so answer b is unacceptable. Answers c and d try to define PriceRange as a subrange type, but a subrange type definition cannot use real values (0.00 and 10000.00). Answer d also has PriceRange and Computers switched in the definition. Answer e does not use Standard Pascal syntax, as the enumerated type definition must precede the use of the type. Thus, only a is left.

3–4. e. The order of the definition of the arrays does not match that of the given definition and/or the syntax is incorrect in the first four answers.

3–5. a. Since there is only one array defined, and that is in taxes, it would be best suited for different taxes for each employee, but not different salaries.

3–6. e. Notice that in a, Loop is an enumerated type, and thus cannot be WRITELNed. In b, parentheses are used instead of the proper square brackets. In c, Tax is a type definition and thus not allowed as a subscript. In d, again Tax is a type definition and not a variable. Thus, only e is left.

3–7. c. VAR definitions do not use equal signs, so a is incorrect. In b, the difference of two type identifiers is not allowed. The format for defining arrays in VAR definitions is incorrect in d and e, so only c is left.

3–8. d. In a, Car is the TYPE needed as a subscript, but not a valid subscript in itself. The same goes for b. In e, Car is not a variable, so it cannot be WRITELNed. In c, the order of the subscripts is inverted, so only d is left.

3–9. a. The text of a book is better suited to files, continuously growing data need linked lists, and the GROUPING of many related items are best suited to records. The ordered storage of values for later searching is handled best by trees.

3–10. e. Answer a needs an expression of TYPE Element as a subscript. In b, Element is the TYPE identifier, not a variable. In c, the problem is the same as was the case with b; plus, it has the added mistake of parentheses instead of square brackets. The lack of square brackets in d is the only problem. Thus, only e could be correct.

3–11. c. The order in which the subranges appear in the subscripts is the determining factor. (The enumerated TYPE Classes corresponds to a subrange 1 .. 4.) Hence, the order in which they appear in the given definition is [1 .. 4], [1 .. 35], [1 .. 10]. Thus the correct answer is c.

3–12. e. Pascal does not allow read and/or write operations on unpacked arrays of characters.

3–13. d. In a, Alpha is not a variable, but a TYPE identifier, so that would cause an error. In b, the same problem applies—Name is another TYPE identifier, not a variable. In c, an attempt is made to read in an array of strings, which is illegal in Pascal. In e, square brackets are needed around Middle—not parentheses. Only in d is there a valid Pascal statement—it will read in a character from the console.

3–14. e. In a, a subrange is not valid in the body of a Pascal program— subranges are only used in TYPE and VARiable definitions. In b, the two sides of the equation are of incompatible types—the left is an array (string), and the right is a single character. In c, subranges are again invalid in the body of a Pascal program. Answer d tries to add two characters, which would be valid if the type on the left side of the equation was a string (of packed array of two charcters), but it's not. Only e has a valid Pascal statement—the two sides of the equation are of the same type.

3–15. c. FullName is an array of Alpha. It has three elements, named First, Middle, and Last. Thus, it contains the equivalent of three variables of type Alpha. Alpha is a packed array of 10 characters. Thus, FullName can contain up to 3 * 10 = 30characters.

3–16. d. The problem here is simply the format of the predefined type String. It takes one subscript, which is its maximum length—not a subrange. There is no dollar sign, either. Thus, the proper answer is d.

3–17. e. First, let's consider what information we have to take care of. We have 10 first names, 10 middle names, and 10 last names— thirty names in all. Convenience dictates that some sort of array be used, as separate variables are simply too difficult to work with. Thus, a and b have been eliminated. Now, if c were used, all 30 names would be in the same string, and a complicated mathematical routine would be necessary to store and retrieve the names. If d were used, there would be 30 strings, but they would not be as easily accessed as if they had been stored as in e, in which an array of an array of strings would allow 10 arrays of 3 strings each—an array of first, middle, and last name for each employee. Thus, e is the best answer.

3–18. e. The text of a book is best handled by files (of characters), a computerized address book best by records, and fast alphabetical storage and retrieval by trees. Number crunching has little, if anything, to do with strings. Thus, e is left.

3–19. d. In d, an attempt to use a subrange in the main body of the Pascal program is made, but that is illegal.

3–20. a. Answers b, d, and e can be eliminated simply because they never define the length of the new concatenation—Final.Length. In answer c, you will notice that the second part of the procedure puts the characters in Second.Data right where the characters from First.Data have been put, thus erasing them. Only a has a working concatenation routine.

3–21. a. The text for a book is best stored in a file; the recording of 100 items of data is best stored in an array (since a fixed number of items is given); three-dimensional graphics processing is also best handled with arrays (since the coordinates can be easily accessed and modified for any shape); and the ordered storage of data for fast access is best handled by a tree. A long list of names, to be kept in alphabetical order, might first be thought best in a tree, but frequent deletion of items from a tree is difficult. Thus, a linked list is best suited to a.

3–22. e. As for answer a, it will cause an error if you try to compile it, as Item is used in its own definition. Answer b contains no way of pointing to the next item in the list from the current Item. Again, c uses Item in its own definition, as does d. Only e constitutes the definition of a linked list. Notice that a linked list does not have to contain a pointer to the preceding item in the linked list (answer e does not do this), but it can, depending on the application.

3–23. e. The first confusion may come as to whether this is a linked list or a binary tree. Although this does have two pointers of item in each record, one is for the NEXT item, and the other is for the PREDecessor in the list, not for two branches of a tree. The next confusion comes as to "What is this a linked list of?" The definition of item contains the two pointers mentioned above and a pointer to a real number. Thus, this must be a linked list of pointers to real numbers, or answer e.

3–24. d. Answer a is an invalid Pascal statement, as NIL is a pointer type, and List is of type Item, since List is a pointer to Item. Answer b is also illegal, as the caret should come after the identifiers (the carets only come before the identifiers in the definitions). In answer e, the predefined procedure New takes a variable of a pointer type as an argument, not of type Item, which is what you get with the caret after the word List. Both c and d have valid syntax, but c does not define List.Pred, which will cause problems later in the program if a reverse search through the list is done. Thus, d is the BEST answer.

3–25. a. In answers b and d, you will find the comparison (Passed = FALSE), which is illegal. This is because Passed is of type REAL, whereas FALSE is a BOOLEAN value. In answers c and d, you will find that A is defined as type Item, but in the program, A is used, thus meaning that A should be a pointer. In d and e, you will find that the ELSE clause in the IF . . . THEN(. . . ELSE) statement is missing, and thus A is never advanced through the list—it keeps checking the same item again and again. Only a has a working version of the desired function.

3–26. b. In answer a, List.Data is of type REAL, but Count is defined as an integer—thus, this is an illegal assignment. In c, Count (an integer), is assigned to P.Data, which is a pointer to a REAL number—again, an illegal assignment. In d and e, variables of type REAL and Item, respectively, are assigned to pointers—which, once again, is invalid, as the types don't match. Only b contains a valid assignment—both sides are pointers to dynamic variables of type Item.

3–27. d. In a, a linked list has only one node per tree (an optional pointer to the preceding item is not considered a node), and a binary tree has only two. Answer b and answer c are possible configurations, but not necessarily true. Answer e is incorrect, as a linked list and a binary tree both have the ability to grow indefinitely (limited only by the computer's memory). Only d is correct.

3–28. b. In a, two elements B and A' are coming off A, so we can immediately eliminate it. In c, you might consider there to be two linked lists, both terminating on B, but the question asks for a single linked list. Answer d has two elements coming off C, so it is not a linked list. Answer e follows the same reasoning, as two elements (or nodes) are coming off B. Only b has each item pointing to one other item.

3–29. d. In the above example, all the shown example definitions are valid except d, because the caret should be on the other side of A. A caret on the left side of the A denotes the dynamic variable pointed to by A, whereas a caret on the right side denotes a type definition of a pointer of type A.

3–30. b. Answer b does not contain a pointer to point to the next node in the list. Thus, it could not be used as a node itself, as each node in a linked list must point to another node.

3–31. e. In this example, 10 is pushed onto the stack, then 2. Add(2) causes the last value on the stack (2) to be popped, added to its argument (2), and the sum (4) is pushed twice. Now the stack has a 10 on the bottom with two 4s on top. The last line in this example then evaluates Popper, which will pop the two 4s and add them. This sum (8) is subtracted from the number popped (10). Thus, 10 − 8 = 2.

3–32. d. This pushes 10, then pushes 10 again. Popper, though, pops both of these values, giving us an empty stack again. It then pushes 2, but the subtract routine pops it right back, so the stack is still empty. Now we push 123, and the add procedure pops this, but pushes the sum (126) onto the stack twice. The last add call pops 1 of these 126s, but also leaves 1, and pushes its own sum (127) twice. Thus, there are 3 numbers on the stack after all this.

3–33. b. In the first line, there are 2 calls to Popper, 1 to subtract, and 1 to add. Thus, 6 numbers are popped from the top of the stack, and 2 are put back onto it. The next line pops these 2, but the first value on the stack has never been touched. Thus, the value still on the stack is a 1.

3–34. b. The first item pushed onto a stack is the last thing to be popped from that stack.

3–35. d. First, 124 is pushed twice, and then 342, so we have 4 numbers on the stack. Add then removes 2 of these, and replaces 1 of them with their sum, for a total of 3 numbers on the stack. Then 12 is pushed twice and 2 is pushed twice, for a new total of 7 numbers. Add then removes 2 of these again, and replaces 1, leaving 6 numbers on the stack. Then 2 is pushed twice again, putting 8 numbers on the stack. Multiply, and the 2 Add calls, each pop 2 numbers, and replace only 1 of them, so the maximum size of the stack is 8 numbers.

3–36. c. First, 12 is pushed onto the stack twice, then both values are popped by Add, and their sum (24) is pushed back onto the stack.

We then push 12 twice more onto the stack, and 1 of these is immediately popped by the Pop function. Then Add pops the remaining 2 values (12 and 24), adds them, and pushes their sum (36). Thus, the remaining number on the stack is 36.

3–37. c. First, Push pushes a 1 onto the stack twice, and then Push pushes 2 onto the stack twice. Since we are only interested in the total number of push operations, we can ignore the Pop operations of the Add procedure. Thus, both of the Add procedures push 1 number onto the stack. The total, then, is 2 + 2 + 1 + 1 = 6.

3–38. c. The first 5 lines push a 1 onto the stack 10 times. Then each of the Add procedure calls will take 2 numbers from the stack and put their sum back onto the stack, so the total of the numbers on the stack is not changed. Thus, after these 5 calls, there are five 1s and one 5 on the stack. Multiply takes the 5 and one of the 1s, multiplies them, and puts the product back on the stack. Thus, we lost a total of 6 from the stack, and only 5 were replaced. Thus, we have a net loss of 1 number. Since there were 10 initially, the final sum of the numbers on the stack must be 9.

3–39. b. In a computer's stack, you never work from the bottom of the stack, only the top. Hence, answers a and c are eliminated. Also, since the very top is ALL you can work with, answer e is also eliminated. Pushing corresponds to adding something new to the stack, so the answer must be b.

3–40. d. By the same reasoning as in the previous problem, answers a, c, and e may be eliminated. Since popping takes away the most recent element pushed on a stack, answer d must be the correct choice.

3–41. b. In a queue, the law of FIFO holds, or first in, first out. This means that the first item placed on a queue is the first item retrieved. The second is the second, and so on. This is very similar to the first come, first served basis of waiting on people in a store.

3–42. c. A queue and a stack are not at all interchangeable. Thus, a must be incorrect. Keeping track of a savings and checking account would not require a queue, just a simple real number. As for inventory control, the first thing shipped into a company is not necessarily the first thing to go out, so a queue would be fairly useless. A dictionary requires the words to be in some sort of order, not just in the order in which they were added. Only c is a good answer. The first thing a computer is asked to do is the first thing it does. If it is asked to do 10 other things while it is still doing the first one, then it will do those 10 things in the order in which they were requested, one after another.

3–43. e. To find the proper answer, let's first examine what must be done to get an item from a queue. Since the queue points to the first item in the queue, we wish to take that item and return it through the function. We also need to redefine the starting point of the queue, though, as the first item has been used. Thus, what was the second item now must become the first. The second item is pointed to by the field Next, so if we make the queue point to that, we will have taken care of redefining the queue. Answers a and b are not even close to doing this; c, d, and e are the only possibilities. If we look closely at d, though, we find it redefines the queue before getting the data, which means that the data we get would actually be the second piece of data, not the first. In e, QueueName is passed as a VARiable parameter, which means if the function changes it, as it does, the change is made to whatever variable was actually passed to the function. In c, the change only occurs locally to the function, which means once the computer returns to the calling body, QueueName is unchanged, and thus is still pointing at the first piece of data in the queue. Thus, e must be the correct answer.

3–44. e. Again, let's first consider what must be done in order to add an INTEGER to our queue. The first thing added to a queue is the first thing out, so it is on top. Thus, the last thing added to a queue, or the most recent, must be on the bottom, or the last thing in the queue. Answers a through d all try to add the new data at the top of the queue. Only e adds it to the bottom.

3–45. a. In answer b, we find that QueueName is changed when this procedure is run, and since it was a VARiable parameter, that means whatever variable was passed has been changed. The procedure was really only to add a number to the queue, though, and to do that, you don't modify the pointer to the top of the queue; you simply add to the bottom of the queue. Thus, b is wrong. Notice in c the condition (QueueName ⟨⟩ NIL). But the value of QueueName is never changed. Thus, this would become an infinite loop if QueueName actually points to something. Answer c must therefore be wrong. Notice that in d, the call to AddToQueue uses QueuePointer as an argument, but the loop just above that had run until QueuePointer had become NIL. Thus, a NIL pointer is passed to AddToQueue, which will not be able to add a number to a non-existent queue. Notice in e that in the first statement in the WHILE loop the value of QueueName.Data is added to the Summation—

but QueueName is never varied. Thus, the same value is added to the sum again and again. Only answer a has the proper format.

3–46. a. First, 2 is put onto the queue. Then Add takes the 2 off the queue, adds 3 to it, and puts the sum (5) back on the queue. Subtract takes the number on top of the queue (5), subtracts it from its own argument (6), and returns the difference (1). Thus, Answer is equal to 1.

3–47. d. First, 2 is put onto the queue. Then a 4 is put on the queue. Add takes the first number on the queue (2), adds it to 5, and puts the sum (7) back on the queue. So now the queue looks like (4, 7). In the next line, Subtract takes the 4 from the top of the queue, subtracts it from 10, and puts the difference (6) back on the queue. Now the queue looks like (7, 6). In the final line, Take takes the number on the top of the queue (7), and puts it in Answer. Thus, the answer is d.

3–48. d. First, a 1 is put on the queue, then a 2, and finally a 3. The queue thus looks like (1, 2, 3), with the 1 on top. Add takes the number on top (1), adds it to 4, and puts the sum (5) back on the queue. Thus, the queue would look like (2, 3, 5), since the 5 would be put on the bottom. Subtract then takes the 2, subtracts it from 5, and returns the difference (3). Take returns the next number on the queue, which would now be a 3. Thus, Answer becomes 3 + 3 = 6. After this, though, (5) is still on the queue, and this is what the question asks for. Thus d is the correct answer.

3–49. a. In a computer's queue, every new item added becomes the last thing to do, so it is placed last on the queue, or on the bottom. Thus, a corresponds to the action of adding another number onto the queue.

3–50. d. In a queue, the next item retrieved is the item that has been there the longest, or put there first. Since you add to the bottom of the pile, whatever was put on the pile first would still be on the top. Thus, you would take the sheet of paper on top—answer d.

3–51. a. The root of this binary tree is A.
b. The leaves are C, E, F, and G.c. The sets of siblings for this tree are B and C, D and E, and F and G.
d. The children of the root are B and C.

3–52. a. 1
b. 1
c. 2
d. 5
e. 12

3-53.

a.　O

b.　X

c.　X　　and　　X

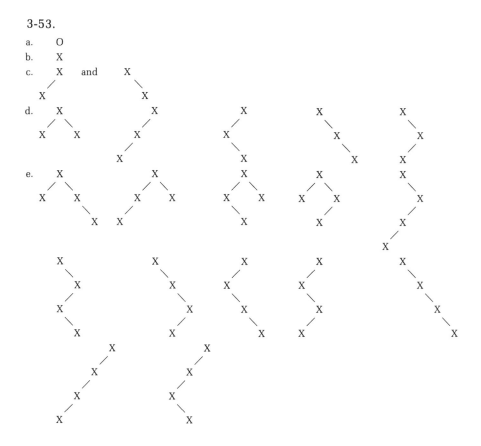

CHAPTER 4 ANSWERS

4–1. The following steps are involved in the bubble sort.

    a. Compare the first item in the list with each successive item.

    b. If the items are out of order, then exchange the values.

    c. Repeat steps a and b, above, comparing every item with every other item.

4–2. The following steps are involved in the insertion sort.

    a. Place the first item from the unsorted list into a new list.

    b. Compare each successive item from the unsorted list to the members of the new list, inserting these items in the list where appropriate.

```
4-3. PROGRAM Bubble (INPUT, OUTPUT);

       CONST
         MaxSubscript = 10;

       VAR
         A : ARRAY [1 .. MaxSubscript] OF INTEGERS;
         OuterCounter, InnerCounter : INTEGER;

     PROCEDURE SwitchValues
       (VAR FirstValue, SecondValue : INTEGER);

       VAR
         Trash : INTEGER;

       BEGIN (* SwitchValues *)
         Trash := FirstValue;
         FirstValue := SecondValue;
         SecondValue := Trash
       END (* SwitchValues *);

     BEGIN (* Bubble *)
       FOR OuterCounter := 1 TO MaxSubscript DO
         BEGIN (* Initialization Loop *)
           WRITE ('What is the value of element ',
             OuterCounter:3);
           READLN (A[OuterCounter])
         END (* Initialization Loop *);
       FOR OuterCounter := 1 TO MaxSubscript - 1 DO
         FOR InnerCounter := OuterCounter - 1 TO MaxSubscript DO
           IF (A[OuterCounter]) < A[InnerCounter])
             THEN Switch (A[OuterCounter], A[InnerCounter]);
       FOR OuterCounter := 1 TO MaxSubscript DO
         WRITELN ('Element ',OuterCounter:3, ' = ',
           A[OuterCounter])
     END. (* Bubble *)


4-4. PROGRAM Insertion (INPUT, OUTPUT);

       CONST
         MaxSubscript := 10;
```

```
TYPE
    Q : ARRAY [1 .. MaxSubscript] OF INTEGERS;

VAR
    A, B : Q;
    OriginalSubscript, NewSubscript, HighestSubscript
        : INTEGER;

PROCEDURE MoveContents
    (VAR HighestSubscript : INTEGER;
        B : ARRAY [1 .. MaxSubscript] OF INTEGER);

VAR
    Subscript : INTEGER;

    BEGIN (* MoveContents *)
    FOR Subscript := HighestSubscript DOWNTO NewSubscript DO
        B[Subscript + 1] := B[Subscript];
    HighestSubscript := HighestSubscript + 1
    END (* MoveContents *);

BEGIN (* Insertion *)
    FOR OriginalSubscript := 1 TO MaxSubscript DO
        BEGIN (* Initialization Loop *)
            WRITE ('What is the value of element ',
                OriginalSubscript:3);
            READLN (A[OriginalSubscript])
        END (* Initialization Loop *);
    OriginalSubscript := 1;
    HighestSubscript := 1;
    NewSubscript := 1;
    B[NewSubscript] := A[OriginalSubscript];
    FOR OriginalSubscript := 2 TO MaxSubscript DO
        FOR NewSubscript := 1 TO HighestSubscript DO
        IF A[OriginalSubscript] = ) B[NewSubscript]
            THEN MoveContents (HighestSubscript, B);
    FOR NewSubscript := 1 TO MaxSubscript DO
        WRITELN ('Element ', NewSubscript:3, ' = ',
            B[NewSubscript])
END. (* Insertion *)
```

4–5. PROGRAM PairExchange (INPUT, OUTPUT);

```
    CONST
      MaxSubscript = 10;

    VAR
      A : ARRAY [1 .. MaxSubscript] OF INTEGER;
      Sorted : BOOLEAN;
      PassCounter, Subscript : INTEGER;

    PROCEDURE SwitchValues
      (VAR Sorted : BOOLEAN;
        FirstValue, SecondValue : INTEGER);

    VAR
      Trash : INTEGER;

    BEGIN (* SwitchValues *)
      Trash := FirstValue;
      FirstValue := SecondValue;
      SecondValue := Trash
    END (* SwitchValues *);

    BEGIN (* PairExchange *)
      FOR Subscript := 1 TO MaxSubscript DO
        BEGIN (* FOR Loop *)
          WRITE ('What is the value of element ',
            Subscript:3);
          READLN (A[Subscript])
        END (* FOR Loop *);
      PassCounter := 1;
      REPEAT
        Sorted := TRUE;
          IF (PassCounter MOD 2 = 1)
            THEN FOR Subscript := 1 TO MaxSubscript DO
              IF (A[Subscript] A[Subscript + 1]
                THEN Switch (Sorted, A[Subscript],
                A[Subscript + 1]);
          IF (PassCounter MOD 2 = 0)
            THEN FOR Subscript := 2 TO MaxSubscript − 1 DO
```

```
            IF (A[Subscript] ⟩ A[Subscript + 1]
                THEN Switch (Sorted, A[Subscript],
                    A[Subscript + 1]);
        PassCounter := PassCounter + 1
    UNTIL Sorted = TRUE;
    FOR Subscript := 1 TO MaxSubscript DO
        WRITELN ('Element ', Subscript:3, ' = ',
            A[Subscript]:1)
    END. (* PairExchange *)
```

4–6.
```
PROGRAM QuickSort (INPUT, OUTPUT);

    CONST
        MaxSubscript = 10;

    VAR
        A : ARRAY [1 .. MaxSubscript] OF INTEGER;
        Pivot, Subscript, First, Last : INTEGER;

    PROCEDURE LastSwitch
        (VAR A[First − 1], A[Last], Last, First : INTEGER);

        BEGIN (* LastSwitch *)
            A[First − 1] := A[Last];
            Last := Last − 1
        END (* LastSwitch *);

    PROCEDURE FirstSwitch
        (VAR A[First], A[Last + 1], First, Last : INTEGER);

        BEGIN (* FirstSwitch *)
            A[Last + 1] := A[First];
            First := First + 1
    END (* FirstSwitch *);

    BEGIN (* QuickSort *)
        FOR Subscript := 1 TO MaxSubscript DO
            BEGIN (* Initialization Loop *)
                WRITE ('What is the value of element ',
                    Subscript:3);
```

```
        READLN (A[Subscript])
      END (* Initialization Loop *);
    Pivot := A[ROUND(MaxSubscript/2)];
    FOR Subscript := ROUND(MaxSubscript/2) − 1
      DOWNTO 1 DO
      A[Subscript + 1] := A[Subscript];
    First := 2;
    Last := MaxSubscript;
    WHILE ((Last - First) 1) DO
      BEGIN (* WHILE Loop *)
        WHILE A[Last] 〉 Pivot DO
          Last := Last − 1;
        LastSwitch (A[First − 1], A[Last], Last, First);
        WHILE A[First] 〉 Pivot DO
          First := First + 1;
        END (* WHILE Loop *);
      FOR Subscript := 1 TO MaxSubscript DO
        WRITELN ('Element ', Subscript:3, ' = ',
        A[Subscript]:1)
  END. (* QuickSort *)



4−7. PROGRAM Radix (INPUT, OUTPUT);

    CONST
      MaxSubscript = 10;

    VAR
      A, C : ARRAY [1 .. MaxSubscript] OF INTEGER;

      B : ARRAY [1 .. MaxSubscript, 1 .. MaxSubscript]
        OF INTEGER;
      R, T, MaxDigit, Counter, SCounter, TCounter : INTEGER;
    BEGIN (*Radix *)
      T := 0;
      FOR Counter := 1 TO MaxSubscript DO
        BEGIN (* FOR Loop *)
          READLN (A[Counter]);
          IF A[Counter] 〉 T
            THEN T := A[Counter]
```

```
          END (* FOR Loop *);
      MaxDigit := 0;
      WHILE T > 0 DO
        BEGIN (* WHILE Loop *)
          T := T DIV 10;
          MaxDigit := MaxDigit + 1
        END (* WHILE Loop *);
      REPEAT
        FOR Counter := 1 TO MaxSubscript DO
          C[Counter] := 1;
        R := 10;
        FOR Counter := 1 TO MaxSubscript DO
        BEGIN (* FOR Loop *)
          B[(A[Counter] MOD R) DIV (R / 10), C[Counter]]
            := A[Counter];
          C[Counter := C[Counter] + 1
        END (* FOR Loop *);
        R := R * 10;
        FOR Counter := 1 TO MaxSubscript DO
          FOR SCounter := 1 TO C[Counter] DO
            A[Counter] := B[Counter, SCounter];
        MaxDigit := MaxDigit - 1
      UNTIL MaxDigit = 0
    END. (* Radix *)


4-8. PROGRAM Selection (INPUT, OUTPUT);
     CONST
       MaxSubscript = 10;
       MAXINT = 32767;

     VAR
       ASubscript, BSubscript, CSubscript, Smallest : INTEGER;
       A, B : ARRAY [1 .. MaxSubscript] OF INTEGER;

     BEGIN (* Selection *)
       FOR ASubscript := 1 TO MaxSubscript DO
         BEGIN (* Initialization Loop *)
           WRITE ('What is the value of element ',ASubscript:3);
           READLN (A[ASubscript])
         END (* Initialization Loop *);
```

```
      BSubscript := 1;
      FOR ASubscript := 1 TO MaxSubscript - 1 DO
        BEGIN (* A Loop *)
          Smallest := A[ASubscript];
          Subscript := ASubscript;
          FOR CSubscript := ASubscript + 1 TO MaxSubscript DO
            IF Smallest < A[CSubscript]
              THEN BEGIN (* Found Smaller Value *)
                Smallest := A[CSubscript];
                Subscript := CSubscript
                END (Found Smallest Value *);
          B[BSubscript] := Smallest;
          BSubscript := BSubscript + 1;
          A[Subscript] := MAXINT
        END (* A Loop *);
      FOR BSubscript := 1 TO MaxSubscript DO
        WRITELN ('Element ', BSubscript:1, ' = ', B[BSubscript])
    END. (* Selection *)
```

4–9. PROGRAM Shell (INPUT, OUTPUT);

```
    CONST
      MaxSubscript = 10;

    VAR
      A : ARRAY [1 .. MaxSubscript] OF INTEGER;
      Differential, Subscript : INTEGER;

    PROCEDURE Switch
      (VAR Subscript, Differential, A[Subscript],
          A[Subscript + Differential] : INTEGER);

      VAR
        Trash : INTEGER;
      BEGIN (* Switch *)
        Trash := A[Subscript];
        A[Subscript] := A[Subscript + Differential];
        A[Subscript + Differential] := Trash
      END (* Switch *);
```

```
BEGIN (* Shell *)
  Differential := TRUNC(MaxSubscript / 2);
  FOR Subscript := 1 TO Differential DO
    IF A[Subscript] > A[Subscript + Differential]
      THEN Switch (Subscript, Differential, A[Subscript],
        A[Subscript + Differential]);
  WHILE Differential > 0 DO
    BEGIN (* WHILE Loop *)
      Differential := TRUNC(Differential / 2);
      FOR Subscript := 1 TO MaxSubscript - 1 DO
        IF A[Subscript] > A[Subscript + Differential]
          THEN Switch (Subscript, Differential,
            A[Subscript], A[Subscript + Differential]9
    END (* WHILE Loop *);
  FOR Subscript := 1 TO MaxSubscript DO
    WRITELN ('Element ', Subscript:3, ' = ',
      A[Subscript]:1)
END. (* Shell *)
```

4–10.
```
PROGRAM Merge (Alpha, Beta, Gamma);

CONST
  MaxSubscript = 10;

VAR
  Alpha, Beta, Gamma : TEXT;
  Done : BOOLEAN;
  A, B : ARRAY [1 .. MaxSubscript] OF REAL;
  C : ARRAY [1 .. 2 * MaxSubscript] OF REAL;
  ASubscript, BSubscript, CSubscript : INTEGER;

BEGIN (* Merge *)

  (* Load Array A *)
  ASubscript := 1;
  RESET (Alpha);
  WHILE NOT EOF (Alpha) DO
    BEGIN (* WHILE Loop *)
      READLN (Alpha, A[ASubscript]);
```

```
        ASubscript := ASubscript + 1
      END (* WHILE Loop *);

    (* Load Array B *)
    BSubscript := 1;
    RESET (Beta);
    WHILE NOT EOF (Beta) DO
      BEGIN (* WHILE Loop *)
        READLN (Beta, B[BSubscript]);
        BSubscript := BSubscript + 1
      END (* WHILE Loop *);

    (* Load Array C *)
    ASubscript := 1;
    BSubscript := 1;
    CSubscript := 1;
    Done := FALSE;
    WHILE Done = FALSE DO
      BEGIN (* WHILE Loop *)
        REPEAT
          C[CSubscript] := A[Asubscript];
          ASubscript := ASubscript + 1;
          CSubscript := CSubscript + 1
        UNTIL (A[ASubscript] > B[BSubscript]) OR
          (ASubscript > MaxSubscript);
        REPEAT
          C[CSubscript] := B[BSubscript];
          BSubscript := BSubscript + 1;
          CSubscript := CSubscript + 1
        UNTIL (B[BSubscript] > A[ASubscript]) OR
          (BSubscript > MaxSubscript);
        IF CSubscript > 2 * MaxSubscript
          THEN Done := TRUE
      END;

    (* Write to file Gamma *)
    REWRITE (Gamma);
    FOR CSubscript := 1 TO 2 * MaxSubscript DO
      WRITELN (Gamma, C[CSubscript])
END. (* Merge *)
```

4–11. b

4–12. a

4–13. a

4–14. b

4–15. e

4–16. d

4–17. b

4–18. a

4–19. c

4–20. b. In Pascal, the ROUND FUNCTION returns the INTEGER nearest to its argument. When the fractional part of the parameter is exactly 0.5, then the number is rounded up if it is positive and down if it is negative. TRUNC, on the other hand, simply removes the fractional part of the REAL number, returning only the INTEGER part. Thus, if a positive number is normally ROUNDed up, it is 0.5 or less away from the INTEGER to which it is rounded. On the other hand, if it is not normally rounded up, then it is more than 0.5 away from the next INTEGER. Thus, if we add 0.5 to a positive number and TRUNCate it instead of ROUNDing it, we have the same result. Thus, the proper answer is b.

4–21. a. Do whatever is inside the parentheses first. Hence, we simplify as follows:

ROUND(1.5 + TRUNC(− 9.9999))

Now, the TRUNCate FUNCTION simply drops the decimal part of the argument, so we now have:

ROUND(1.5 + (− 9))
ROUND(−7.5)

The ROUND FUNCTION rounds its argument to the nearest IN-TEGER. If the fractional part of the argument is exactly 0.5, then it is rounded up if the argument is positive and down if the argument is negative. Our argument is negative (-7.5), so it is rounded down to -8, answer a.

4–22. c. To make sure that the expression returns a number within our desired endpoints, we simply check the extremes of the possible values that RandomNumber may return. In a, if RandomNumber = 0, then the whole expression would equal zero. The same goes for b. Thus, a and b cannot be the expressions we are after. In d, if RandomNumber = 0, then the entire expression equals ROUND(100 * 0 + 1), or 1, so it is in our lower boundary. But if RandomNumber is very close to 1, say for example 0.999, we find the expression returns ROUND(100 * 0.999 + 1) = ROUND(99.9 + 1) = ROUND(100.9). We find that this value is rounded up to 101, which is out of our range. In e, if RandomNumber returns 0.999, we find the expression returns TRUNC(100 * (0.999 + 1)) = TRUNC(100 * 1.999) = TRUNC(199.9) = 199, which is not even close to our desired range. In c, though, if RandomNumber returns a zero, we get TRUNC(100 * 0 + 1) = TRUNC(1) = 1, which is the bottom of our range. And if RandomNumber returns a number very close to 1, say 0.999, then we get TRUNC(100 * 0.999 + 1) = TRUNC(99.9 + 1) = TRUNC(100.9). When the decimal is dropped off by the TRUNC FUNCTION, this will return 100, which is the top of our desired range. Hence, c is the answer.

4–23. a. Refer to question 4–20 above, to confirm that TRUNC(X + 0.5) = ROUND(X) whenever X is positive or zero. Now, Z2 is the square of a real number, and so it is positive for all real numbers. Thus, the rule TRUNC(X + 0.5) = ROUND(X) holds for X = Z2, so TRUNC(Z2 + 0.5) = ROUND(Z2) all the time.

4–24. e. If we try Z = -1, we find TRUNC((-1)3 + 0.5) = TRUNC(-0.5) = 0, and ROUND((-1)3) = ROUND(-1) = -1. Thus, it doesn't work for all negative numbers, and we can eliminate answers a and c. On the other hand, if Z = -0.1, then TRUNC((-0.1)3 + 0.5) = TRUNC(-0.001 + 0.5) = TRUNC(0.499) = 0, and ROUND((-0.1)3) = ROUND(-0.001) = 0, so it does work for some negative numbers. Thus, answers b and d are also wrong. Answer e is then the only proper choice.

4–25. e. If Money(15) is the amount of interest after 15 years, all we have to do is find a way to round it to two decimal places (since we have to round it to the nearest penny). If we multiply Money(15) by 100, the hundred's column is moved to the one's column. Here, the ROUND function can round it off properly for us. After we ROUND this, though, we must remember to divide this by 100 to get it back to the same magnitude as we originally had. Thus, our expression looks like this: ROUND(Money(15) * 100) / 100—which is what we find in answer e.

4–26. e. Choice a will produce $-3 + -3 = -6$; choice b will produce $-3 + -4 = -7$. In choice c, we have $-3 + 0 = -3$, whereas in choice d we have $-3 + -34/10 = -3 + -3.4 = -6.4$. Only choice e will produce $-3 + -4/10 = -3.4$.

4–27. a. To round a number to X places, we first want to move that column or place into the one's column. To move the first decimal column into the one's column, we multiply by 10, or 10^1 (for the second, 10^2, and so on). Thus, we want to multiply Y by 10^X before we round it off. After the rounding is done, we then need to divide by the same thing—10^X—so that we have the same magnitude number that we had before. Thus, the expression in a is the one we are after.

4–28. c. Remember that ROUND(X) rounds X up whenever the fractional part is greater than or equal to 0.5 (for a positive X). TRUNC(X) always cuts off the fractional part of X. ROUND(X) drops the fractional part, too, when the fractional part of X is less than 0.5. Thus, they both return X without its fractional part when that fractional part is less than 0.5.

4–29. e. If $X = 3.6$, then choice a is false:

$$\text{TRUNC(ROUND(3.6))} = 4 \quad 3 = \text{ROUND(TRUNC(3.6))}.$$

If $X = -0.6$, then choice b is false:

$$\text{TRUNC(ROUND}(-0.6)) = -1 \quad 0 = \text{ROUND(TRUNC}(-0.6 + 0.5)).$$

If $X = 1.1$, then choice c is false:

$$\text{TRUNC(ROUND(1.1} + 0.5)) = 2 \quad 1 = \text{ROUND(1.1)}.$$

If $X = 1.1$, then choice d is false:

$$\text{TRUNC(1.6)} = 1 \quad 2 = \text{ROUND(TRUNC(1.6} + 0.5)).$$

Note: These are not the only values for which these four expressions are not true, but by showing that they do not hold for any particular value, we have shown that they are not true in general. Thus, the answer is e.

4–30. d. Each time the loop is passed through, the difference between the LowerLimit and the UpperLimit is halved. The loop runs until this difference is less than Error, so the answer to the question is the same as "How many times do you have to divide 10 by 2 so that the final quotient is less than 0.1?" (We get the 10 from the original difference between the limits: 10 − 0 = 10.) Thus, if you work it out, you will find that the answer is 7.

4–31. c. The second line "Count := 0;" is only executed if the loop has been passed through 100 times without getting close enough to the root. If this happens, then count is set to zero by this statement, the loop is terminated, and the fact that Count = 0 keeps the rest of the program from printing the message that a zero has been located to the function. Thus, it is acting as a flag to the rest of the program.

4–32. c. If the limits are typed into the computer in the wrong order, the computer still goes on and enters the loop initially. It averages the two limits and tests to see which side of the zero the average of the numbers falls on. If the average falls above the zero of the function, it replaces UpperLimit, but UpperLimit actually contained the lower of the two limits. The same is true if it falls below the zero of the function—you have two values both less than the zero. So the zero is no longer between the two limits the computer has to work with. Further, the larger of the two limits is LowerLimit, so when the computer comes to the end of the first loop, (UpperLimit − LowerLimit) will be negative, so it will be less than Error, and the loop will end. Thus, the program will report having found a root between two numbers after one loop, but it won't actually be there. Thus, c is the correct answer.

4–33. c. If there is no root contained in the limits that the computer is given, the computer will still continue to go through the loop each time and average the two limits. If there is no root IN the limits, there must be one on one side and/or the other of these limits. The program will keep replacing the limit that is further away from this root with the average as long as it remains in the loop. Thus, it runs until the difference in the two roots is less than Error, and only one of the two limits will ever be changed. It will then report having found a root. But actually, there is no root in the interval that it will report. Thus, the answer is c.

4–34. d. First, by examination, we see that the only root to this problem is $X = -2$. Using the results of the previous problems, we can say the following: answer a will not work, as there is no root between the limits. And, as the answer to problem 4–33, above, shows, the reported answer will be incorrect. Answer b will also not work, as the LowerLimit is greater than the UpperLimit—problem 4–32 shows why this will not work. Again in c, there is no root contained in the interval, and so the output from the program will again be incorrect. Answer d, on the other hand, has the limits in the proper order, and the root is contained in the limits, so the algorithm will work.

CHAPTER 5 ANSWERS

5–1. b. The procedure Hanoi calls itself—in fact, it calls itself twice. Anything that calls itself is called recursive. This procedure keeps calling itself, each time making Height one smaller until Height is zero. Thus, this program is using a recursive procedure to simplify the task of moving numerous disks down to the task of moving only one disk at a time.

5–2. d. The main program calls it once with Height equal to 4. This, in turn, invokes it twice, each time with Height equal to 3. These invoke it four times, twice for each of the two, with Height equal to 2, then eight times with Height equal to 1. Each of these invokes it twice with Height equal to 0, but none of these continue, as the first line of the procedure ensures. Thus, we have $1 + 2 + 4 + 8 + 16 = 31$.

5–3. c. Each time that the procedure is called, it prints a line of the solution, except when the height passed to the procedure is zero. Thus, the number above (31), the number of times that the height given was zero (16), will be our answer: $31 - 16 = 15$.

5–4. e. The three variables Ignoring, From, and To have nothing to do with which disk is being moved. Thus, the answers a through d cannot possibly be correct.

5–5. a. The first main part varies the column for each given row, thus checking each row to see if it has Tic-Tac-Toe. The next varies the row for each column, thus checking the column. The final one checks for row numbers equal to column numbers, thus checking the diagonal.

5–6. e. The routines that check for rows and/or columns of Tic-Tac-Toe are complete, and if they find one, the fact that a Tic-Tac-Toe was found is saved in the function variable TicTacToe itself, so modifying the variable Temp does not affect that. The diagonal routine, though, only checks for where the row number and the column number are equal, or in other words, from top left to bottom right. It forgets to check for top right to bottom left.

5–7. c. Answer c is correct, for exactly the reason stated in the answer. The rest of the answers make little or no sense.

CHAPTER 6 ANSWERS

6–1. c. The reasoning behind this is basically as follows: Both RAM and ROM are incredibly expensive to use in large quantities. You can store relatively little on a floppy disk, and so, even though they are inexpensive per disk, they are actually quite expensive per byte of storage. Hard disks store a great deal more per disk, but with current technology, it is quite expensive to purchase large quantities of removable hard disks. Only magnetic tapes have, over the years, proven to be a cost efficient method of storing the large amounts of data needed for archiving.

6–2. a. RAM has always been known to be the quickest memory device attached to a computer. The only possible debate here really is between RAN and ROM. The question specified, though, is for the fastest for both storage and retrieval. Although ROM may actually be as fast (if not faster) than RAN in some cases, it takes extended periods of time (up to a few hours) to program ROMs. Thus RAM is really the only choice left.

6–3. d. The microcomputer industry has been using floppy disks for years for a fast mass-storage device. Granted, RAM is also used for fast storage, but the amount of RAM in a machine is normally much less than that on a floppy disk.

6–4. a. Scratch-pad memory is used by a computer to do its messy work, to store a value temporarily, to hold a stack, and so on. For these operations, the quickest possible memory is needed, so as not to slow down the elementary functions of the computer. Thus, RAM is used in scratch-pads.

6–5. e. RAM stores electric pulses in a current. ROM uses either electric pulses similar to RAM or has special circuits built into an integrated circuit. Magnetic tape, as the name implies, uses a magnetic storage method, similar to that found on cassette tapes. Floppy disks and hard disks also use a magnetic storage method, though. There are actually millions of tiny magnets on a disk, and the disk drive "feels" for each of these magnets to see how it is set.

6–6. e.

6–7. e. The definition given to megabyte is one K, or kilobytes. One K is 1024 (in the computer field), so 1024 * 1024 bytes of memory is a megabyte. 1024 * 1024 = 2^{20}. Note: The Latin definition of the prefix *mega* is translated "much, many." Over the years, science has taken this to mean exactly one million, or 10^6. In computer science, in which base 2 is used, we use the numbers above.

Glossary

ACM *See* Association for Computing Machinery.

Actual parameter. The parameter in a subprogram having its value passed to it from elsewhere, such as from a PROCEDURE or FUNCTION.

A/D converter. Converts information from analog to digital form.

ADA. A high-order computer language named after the Countess Lovelace; has its origins in the computer language Pascal.

Address. A location in a computer's memory.

Algorithm. A method for solving a problem; eventually implemented by a computer program.

Alphanumeric. Any combination of letters and numbers.

American National Standards Institute. A body that makes recommendations for greater uniformity in reference to computer languages.

American Standard Code for Information Interchange. A code used in most computers to represent all the possible characters used in a computer. See Appendix for a listing of these characters. ASCII is not used by IBM computers.

AND. A logical operator; causes the computer to compare two words bit by bit.

Annotation. An explanatory note concerning a program or part thereof.

ANSI. *See* American National Standards Institute.

ARRAY. A matrix; in Pascal, this reserved word refers to a type of data structure.

ASCII. *See* American Standard Code for Information Interchange.

Assembler. A computer program that translates an asembler language program into one that can be understood by the computer.

Assembler language. A lower-level computer language consisting of mnemonics as instructions.

Assignment. The process whereby a value is given to a variable or FUNCTION.

Assignment operator. Signifies that a value is to be assigned to a variable; in Pascal, this is symbolized by ":=".

Association for Computing Machinery. The major professional society for computer people.

Asynchronous. An operation whose execution is not tied to some external timing device.

Backplane. A panel into which the printed circuit boards of a computer are plugged.

Backup. A copy of a program.

BASIC. A high-order computer language commonly implemented on microcomputers; stands for Beginner's All-purpose Symbolic Instruction Code.

Batch processing. The execution of a computer program that does not interact with the user.

Baud. The transmission rate of data, usually one bit per second.

BEGIN. Reserved word in Pascal that signals the start of a PROCEDURE, FUNCTION, program body, or any other multiline section.

Benchmark. A standard of comparison.

Binary number system. A system of numbers based on two; consists only of zeros and ones.

Binary tree. A type of tree structure wherein each node leads, maximally, to two branches.

Bit. Binary digit; in the binary number system, it is a zero or a one.

Bomb. The failure of a computer program to execute as intended, quite often with spectacular results.

Boolean data. Data that takes on a "logical" value of either TRUE or FALSE.

Boot. To start up a computer system.

Bottom-up. Analyzing a problem or program from the program code up to the idea behind the program.

Branch. The part of a tree that leads to a node; in practice, it is a pointer.

Bubble sorting algorithm. Involves comparing every element with every other element and exchanging values that are out of the desired order.

Buffer. A temporary storage area for data.

Bug. An error in a computer program.

Byte. Eight bits of information.

CASE. A control structure wherein there are several alternate courses of action which are chosen from during the running of the program.

Central processing unit. The part of a computer that actually does the work of computing.

Central tendency. The probability of data conforming to expected values. ues.

CHAR. A reserved word in Pascal meaning any character.

Character data. Data composed of nonnumeric items (may include numbers but only in a nonmathematical sense).

Child. A node that can be traced back to another node, its parent.

Chip. An integrated circuit.

COBOL. A high-order computer language that is commonly used in business applications; stands for COmmon Business Oriented Language.

Coding. The writing of an algorithm as a computer program.

Command scanner. A program that examines each statement outside of a user-written program.

Comment. A brief message contained in a program; ignored by the computer during program execution; in Pascal, comments are enclosed within square brackets or parenthesis-asterisk pairs.

Compile. The conversion or translation of a high-order computer language into one that is understood by the computer.

Compiler. A computer program that translates a high-order computer language program into one that is understood by the computer.

Computer. A physical device used to carry out stored operations very rapidly.

Computer science. A branch of knowledge dealing with computers and their applications.

Concatenation. String addition, that is, the joining of two or more strings to form a new string.

Conditional execution. The execution of a statement(s) depends on the specified condition(s) being valid (Boolean TRUE).

Conditional statement. A computer statement that consists of a condition and an executable statement; in Pascal, examples include the IF . . . THEN and IF . . . THEN(. . . ELSE) statements.

CONST. A reserved word in Pascal that signifies that which follows deals with the declaration of parameters as constant values.

Constant. Unvarying in value; in Pascal, variables that are not to have their values changed are so declared in the CONST section.

Control Program for Microprocessors. A disk operating system used by the 8080 family of microprocessors.

CPM. *See* Control Program for Microprocessors.

CPS. Characters per second.

CPU. *See* central processing unit.

Crash. The cessation of the operation of a computer.

CRT. Cathode ray tube; used for a visual display by the computer.

Cursor. The mark on a video screen that indicates where the next character will be written.

D/A converter. Converts information from digital to analog form.

Daisy wheel printer. A printer that has a typing head in the shape of a wheel.

Data. The information that is manipulated by a computer.

Data-base management. The maintenance of large amounts of data.

Debug. Correction of errors found within a computer program.

Declaration. Informing the computer of various items of information.

Decrement. To decrease the value of a variable.

Disk. *See* diskette.

Disk drive. Mechanical device used to access diskettes.

Disk operating system. A computer program that controls access to a disk drive.

Diskette. Magnetic recording medium upon which computer data is stored and may be retrieved in a random manner.

Disperison. The extent to which data varies from its expected value.

DIV. A reserved word in Pascal meaning integer division.

DO. A reserved word in Pascal that is followed by a statement or series of statements that are to be executed.

Documentation. An explanation of the purpose of a program or a section of a program; it is for human, not computer use.

DOS. *See* disk operating system.

Dot matrix printer. A printer whose typing head is made up of a series of wires; when used, each character looks like a series of dots.

Double-sided diskette. A diskette that has a recording surface on both sides.

Double-density diskette. A diskette capable of storing twice the amount of data on its recording surface as a single-density diskette.

Double precision. Using two words to represent a number.

Download. To remove data (including a program) from a computer.

DOWNTO. A reserved word in Pascal that causes a decrement of the counter in a FOR loop.

EBCDIC. See Extended Binary Coded Decimal Interchange Code.

Editor. A computer program used to alter files stored by the computer; used when writing computer programs in a noninteractive language, for example, Pascal.

EIA. See Electronics Industry Association.

Electronic mail. Using a computer to deliver messages from one user to another.

Electronics Industry Association. An organization that sets interface standards (for example, RS-232).

ELSE. A reserved word in Pascal that is used in a conditional statement to signify an alternative to the THEN instruction.

END. A reserved word in Pascal that signifies the completion of the statement(s) within a PROCEDURE, FUNCTION, the program body, or any other multiline segment.

End of file. The last item in a file.

End of line. The last item on a line.

EOF. See end of file.

EOLN. See end of line.

Exchange sorting algorithm. Another name for a bubble sorting algorithm.

Execute. To carry out a set of instructions by a computer.

Extended Binary Coded Decimal Interchange Code. Used to represent all the characters used by a computer, most often used on an IBM system.

FALSE. A reserved word in Pascal that has a logical meaning.

FIFO. See first in, first out.

File. A collection of data not stored within a computer program, but which may be used by one.

File-management system. Method of maintaining files so that more than one program may use them.

First in, first out. The handling of information or instructions in the order in which they are received.

Flippy diskette. A diskette that has two recording sides.

Floating-point number. A real number that has a decimal portion and is written using a modified type of scientific notation.

Floppy diskette. A flexible diskette.

Flowchart. A pictorial representation of an algorithm.

FOR. A reserved word in Pascal that signifies the start of a loop.

Formal parameter. Another name for a parameter within a subprogram that receives its value from the main program.

Formatting. Systematizing output to form a desired pattern.

FORTRAN. A high-order computer language used commonly for mathematical and scientific applications; stands for formula translator.

Function. A subprogram that represents a computed value.

Garbage in, garbage out. When a program is written incorrectly or given incorrect information, it cannot produce good results.

GIGO. *See* garbage in, garbage out.

Global identifier. An identifier that has a meaning in the outermost block of a computer program.

GOTO. A reserved word in Pascal that is used as an unconditional branching statement.

Hacker. A person who is not trying to learn about computers in a meaningful manner, but rather by trial and error.

Hard disk drive. A disk drive with a rigid recording medium.

Hard wired. A permanent connection.

Hardware. The physical components of a computer system.

Hexadecimal. A number system based on 16.

High-level computer language. *See* high-order computer language.

High-order computer language. A computer language close to English in its terminology.

High-resolution graphics. Graphics similar in appearance to what they are meant to represent.

Hollerith. Pertains to the use of punched cards by a computer.

Host computer. The central computer in a network of computers.

IC. *See* integrated circuit.

IF. A reserved word in Pascal that is used in a conditional statement and is followed by a condition whose validity must be determined.

IN. An operator that may be used for set membership.

Increment. Increase in value.

Initialize. To set a variable to a particular beginning value.

Input. Putting information into a program from an external source; as an identifier, INPUT refers to obtaining values from the keyboard.

Insertion sorting algorithm. A sorting algorithm that involves placing the unordered items from one array into a second, ordered array.

Integer. A number without a decimal portion.

Integrated circuit. Sometimes referred to as a chip or an IC; essentially consists of computer programs in the form of a piece of hardware.

Interface. Enable two different computers or other devices to communicate with each other, even though they do not "speak" the same language.

Invariant. A constant.

I/O. Input/output.

ISO. International Standards Organization.

ISO Standard Pascal. The version of Pascal as determined by the International Standards Organization.

Iterative algorithm. An algorithm that involves looping; repetitive in nature.

Job. A program submitted to a computer for execution.

Justification. Making the margins of the output even; most text is formatted with the left margin justified; books also have right justification.

K. Kilo; in "computerese", K is 1024, not 1000.

Kludge. An improvised program that does not employ the most elegant algorithm but works nonetheless.

LABEL. A reserved word in Pascal that is used to enable the computer to find a particular statement within a program.

Last in, first out. The execution of instructions or securing of data from a list in the reverse order in which they are found.

Leaf. The terminal node(s) of a tree.

Letter-quality printer. A printer whose output is difficult to distinguish from that of an ordinary typewriter.

LIFO. *See* last in, first out.

Linear search. Examination of all members of a set of data; may be either ordered or unordered.

Linked list. An ordered set of data that makes use of pointers.

Local identifier. An identifier that is defined within a subprogram.

Logic error. An error caused by a mistake in the algorithm.

Loop. A series of instructions that are repeatedly executed.

Low-resolution graphics. Graphics that resemble to a low degree what they are meant to represent.

Machine language. The only language that a computer understands.

Mainframe computer. A very large computer, both in reference to memory as well as to physical size.

Matching. Comparing strings or parts thereof.

Matrix. An array.

MAXINT. The MAXimum INTeger allowed on a computer.

Mega. One million.

Memory. Where a computer stores information.

Merge sorting algorithm. An algorithm wherein the contents of two ordered arrays are combined to form a third, ordered array.

Microcomputer. A small computer, both in reference to memory as well as to physical size.

Minicomputer. An intermediate-sized computer, both in reference to memory as well as to physical size.

Mnemonic. An abbreviation recognized by a computer to mean a particular instruction.

MOD. A reserved word in Pascal that results in the return of the remainder only in a division.

Modeling. Generation of the essence of a problem by a computer.

Modem. A physical device used to allow computers to communicate with each other across telephone lines.

Modularization. The use of independent, self-contained subprograms within a computer program.

Monitor. The visual display device for a computer.

Monte Carlo technique of testing. Random generation of test data, possibly within specific bounds.

Network. An interconnection of computers designed to share resources.

NIL. A reserved word in Pascal that results in a variable having no value, that is, it is "empty."

Node. Where data is stored in a tree.

Noise. A distortion of an electrical signal.

NOT. A reserved word in Pascal that has a logical value.

Number crunching. Long, complex calculations.

Nybble. Four bits.

Octal. A number system based on eight.

OF. A reserved word in Pascal used in the declaration of arrays.

Off line. Not connected to a computer.

On line. Connected to a computer.

Operating system. A computer program that controls the functioning of the various parts of the computer.

Operator. In mathematics, operators are $+$, $-$, $*$, and $/$; in Pascal, DIV, MOD, AND, and OR are added.

OR. A reserved word in Pascal that causes the computer to examine a word bit by bit.

Order of precedence. The hierachy of execution of compound functions.

Ordered tree. A tree that has the arrangement of its nodes determined by a set of criteria.

Ordinal type. An ordered range of values; includes integer, Boolean, and character values, but not real.

Output. The results produced by a computer program; as an identifier, OUTPUT refers to the CRT.

PACKED. A reserved word in Pascal that causes the computer to put several items into a single computer word.

Pair exchange sorting algorithm. A sorting algorithm that involves the comparison of data as arranged in pairs.

Parallel. Transmitting several bits of information at the same point in time.

Parameter. A variable.

Parent. The node of a tree from which further nodes are given off.

Pascal. A high-order computer language named after the French mathematician Blaise Pascal.

Peripheral. Any part of a computer system exclusive of the CPU.

Pointer. A form of data that is used to direct the computer to the next item of data.

Port. An I/O connection.

Pretty printing. Formatting a program or program output so that it is more readable by a human.

Primary memory. The place in a computer where information is stored temporarily, for example, where a program is stored during execution.

Primitive data type. The simplest data form.

PROCEDURE. A form of subprogram.

PROGRAM. A reserved word in Pascal that signifies the actual beginning of a program.

Push. To place an item on a stack.

Queue. A form of data structure that follows the FIFO rule (first in, first out).

Quicksort. A sorting algorithm making use of pivot values.

Radix. The base or root of a number.

Radix sorting algorithm. A sorting algorithm based on the radix of the items being sorted.

Read only memory. The part of a computer's memory that cannot be erased or destroyed.

REAL. A reserved word in Pascal that signifies that a particular parameter has a floating-point value.

RECORD. A reserved word in Pascal that signifies a collection of related information.

Recursion. The process whereby a subprogram calls itself.

Recursive algorithm. An algorithm that involves recursion.

Reference parameter. A parameter not accessed by name, but through a pointer variable.

REPEAT. A reserved word in Pascal that signifies the beginning of a loop.

Reserved word. A word in Pascal for which a meaning has been assigned in the specification of the language; this meaning cannot be changed.

RF modulator. A device that converts the signal from a computer to the type that can be interpreted by a television.

ROM. See read only memory.

Root. The first node of a tree.

Round-off error. An error caused by limitations in the maximal number of digits a computer uses in storing numbers.

Scope of an identifier. The range in a program over which an identifier has a meaning.

Scrolling. The movement of the lines on a video terminal.

Searching time. The amount of time that is required to examine a set of data and return the desired information.

Secondary memory. The place in a computer used for long-term storage of information.

Selection sorting algorithm. A sorting algorithm involving the examination of an unsorted array to pick out successively larger values and assign these values to a second array.

Sequential algorithm. An algorithm that does not involve loops.

Sequential execution. The implementation of a sequential algorithm.

Sequential search. A search whereby each item in a list is examined until the item sought is either found or the end of the list is encountered; the search begins at the beginning of the list and progresses through the list in a FIFO manner.

Serial. The processing of one bit of information at a time.

SET. A reserved word in Pascal.

Sibling. Two nodes coming off the same previous node in a tree.

Simulation. The modeling of a real problem by a computer.

Single-density diskette. A diskette that stores information only on one portion of its recording side.

Single-sided diskette. A diskette that has its recording medium only on one side.

Software. A computer program.

Sorting. The arranging of data into a specified order.

Stack. The place in a computer where partially executed subprograms and their respective variables are stored.

Standard function. In Pascal, these are built-in mathematical operations.

String. A literal; a sequence of characters.

String processing. Manipulations of strings, for example, concatenation, substring extraction, and matching.

Subroutine. A statement or set of statements that may be executed from anywhere within a program.

Substring extraction. The removal of a portion of a string.

Subtree. A tree that has as its root the node of another tree.

Symbolic data. Data represented by variables.

Syntax error. An error caused by a violation of the rules of grammar for the language being used.

System software. A computer program that is used to control the functioning of the computer.

Test data. Data used to verify a program's correctness.

TEXT. A reserved word in Pascal that refers to a type of file.

Text Processing. Manipulation of the contents of a file in a nonmathematical manner.

THEN. A reserved word in Pascal that is used in a conditional statement; If the condition is valid, another command follows.

Time-sharing. The use of a common memory by several terminals simultaneously.

TO. A reserved word in Pascal that is used in a FOR loop; it is preceded by the initial value and followed by the ending value of the parameter being incremented in the loop.

Top-down. Taking a problem and breaking it down into successively smaller problems, each of which can be solved by a section of a program.

Trace. Following the execution of a program line by line; involves the examination of every memory location being changed by the program.

Tree. A data structure that contains nodes with more than one pointer field.

Tree traversal. Visiting all the nodes in a tree in a particular order.

TRUE. A Boolean value.

TYPE. A kind of data definition wherein the list of allowable values is enumerated.

Unordered tree. A tree composed of nodes arranged in a seemingly random order.

UNTIL. A reserved word in Pascal that is used in a REPEAT loop; is followed by a condition that is tested for validity at the end of each pass through the loop.

Value parameter. The variable in a subprogram that takes on a value that is passed to the subprogram.

VAR. A reserved word in Pascal that signifies that which follows are variables whose value may change during the course of the execution of the program.

Variable. An identifier that may change in value over time within a program.

WHILE. A reserved word in Pascal that begins a loop; it is followed by a condition whose validity is checked prior to the execution of the loop on each pass.

WITH. A statement in Pascal that allows the programmer to abbreviate the fields within a record by specifying the record name only once, yet allowing the program to select the field components in question.

Index